Passion@Work

Passion@Work

Be a small business dynamo with
heart, vision, values and passion

Shivani

Hardie Grant Books

Published in 2008
Hardie Grant Books
85 High Street
Prahran, Victoria 3181, Australia
www.hardiegrant.com.au

Cataloguing-in-Publication data is available from the National Library of Australia.
Passion@Work: Be a small business dynamo with heart, vision, values and passion

ISBN 978 1 74066 6459 (Paperback)

Printed and bound in Australia by McPherson's Printing Group

10 9 8 7 6 5 4 3 2 1

Dedication

I would like to dedicate this book to my soulmate and husband Scott who challenges me to grow beyond what I think is possible. And without whom this book would not be a reality, for his support and love is unconditional.

Acknowledgements

To my parents (mum and papa) for always giving me their support in tough times and good and for letting me be me and telling me all was possible.

To Nitin and Ruchi for the great conversations.

To Sebastian and Oliver for teaching me about parenting.

To my friends and particularly to the family of women that guide, mentor and challenge me.

To all the people who have entered my life through work — coaching, workshops, keynote speaking, TV presenting and writing — who I have had a chance to interact with and learn from.

To the spiritual teachers who have guided me through their books and teachings.

To the wonderful people who I was able to interview for this book and who are an inspiration to others.

To Damien for helping conduct the interviews.

To Lisa and Mel for their input into the book.

To Pam and all the staff at Hardie Grant Books who understood my dream for this book and are on this journey with me.

Foreword

Over a working life time, I have seen many young Australians in different walks of life, face significant personal challenges, look for inspiration and then find an inner strength which drives them to succeed in their chosen field. Whether that is in the corporate world, the community sector or on the footy field, I have been blessed to witness the growth and development of many talented individuals.

These experiences have confirmed to me that a person's background is irrelevant, the school they came from, the first job that they had or how many degrees they have. What sets these individuals apart most is their passion to succeed, their immense dedication to their cause, the sacrifices they are prepared to make along the way and their preparedness to seek out help from others.

Through my different positions and experiences I have encounted many talented Australians wanting help in the journey to find their passion and I have been fortunate enough to be in the position to try and contribute something to their journeys.

Shivani is one such talented Australian who I first met when she was doing work with Minter Ellison Lawyers in Adelaide. It became obvious to me that here was a woman who though highly educated in Engineering and having worked in a senior corporate position at a young age was pursuing her passion of running her own business. I remember remarking at the time that whilst it was great she was growing professionally it was critical that she also grow personally in order to achieve business success.

Now nearly four years later, Shivani has indeed embarked on a journey of personal growth and transformation.

In her first book passion@work, Shivani openly shares her journey of self-discovery, leaving the comfort behind and following her dream. In this frank and insightful story Shivani offers the reader the emotion and reality of her experiences, what mistakes she made along the way and many practical suggestions for other small business owners.

Shivani's journey has allowed her to meet other inspiring young Australians, and to inspire and help them to follow their passions. Their honest insights and learnings are kindly offered in this book.

This book is a significant step forward in Shivani's life to achieving her dream of helping and influencing many people both within Australia and beyond.

In this book, you will get a real insight into what it is like to run your own business and what it takes to achieve success. Through these pages I hope it will enable you as the reader to find passion@work.

Wayne Jackson

Chairman Minters Ellison Lawyers

– South Australia & Northen Territory

Former Commissioner & CEO of the Australian Football League

Model the book is based on

Contents

Chapter 1

The journey begins

The start of the journey  Your funeral  Asking for wisdom  Maslow's hierarchy of needs  Vision, values, principles  Reactive and proactive language

If you do not go within –
you go without.
– Ken Wilber, A Brief History of Everything

It's just after 9/11 and most of the world has decided that it's going to stop, and here I am trekking through the Annapurna Ranges in Nepal and I feel completely lost. Afraid not because of 9/11. That is a huge tragedy, hard to describe, hard to get your head around. The images keep coming across on television, in print and everywhere else around us at the moment.

Most of my family and friends were worried about 9/11 and the Nepalese situation and told me, 'don't go to Nepal'. I remember checking with authorities whether it was okay to travel and they said it was, although the Nepalese royal family had just been slain. In spite of this I don't feel afraid of any of the things going on around me.

I don't feel afraid because of 9/11 or the Nepalese environment. What I'm afraid of is who I am. I am really confused. Trekking through Nepal each day gave me time to think finally, away from mobiles, laptops and everything else which made me accessible 24/7. Finally I had some time to myself, and I realised that I did not know who I was.

All my life growing up in an Indian culture, it was so important for me and to my family that I get a really good education. So I went and did that. I completed an engineering degree, I got an MBA and I achieved a senior management role at a young age, which was always my dream.

I reached that peak but it didn't feel like a high. And so here I was walking around in a completely unknown country trying to conquer other peaks, wondering who I really was, in an unhappy relationship and asking where I had gone wrong. Could I have taken different steps? I had postponed my trip to Nepal twice, which was very annoying. Although an opportunity had arisen for my career overseas, I wanted to take my holiday and take some time out.

There are certain moments I experienced in Nepal that are as vivid in my mind as if they are happening in front of me. One day I bought a bag of cheap sugar-lollies. I think the whole bag cost me a dollar and it had about a hundred lollies in it – so they were about a cent per lolly. Nothing special. I carried the lolly bag in my backpack and would unpack it when groups of small kids came over. The kids, not surprisingly, spoke no English or very little besides 'hello' or 'bye'. I would open my lolly bag, take out a sweet and pass one to each child.

One day a boy of about four years old walked up to me, an absolutely beautiful boy. I can still see his face if I close my eyes. I opened up my bag and gave him a lolly and he sucked on it as if his life depended on it. But he sucked it only for a short while and then put it back in the wrapper. I didn't understand.

After a few moments, I realised that the lolly, that one-cent lolly I'd given him, was probably going to give him pleasure for days. He would take little sucks of it in his own time for the sweet pleasure of it and then wrap it back up, just so it'd be there for the next time until eventually it reduced and then completely disappeared.

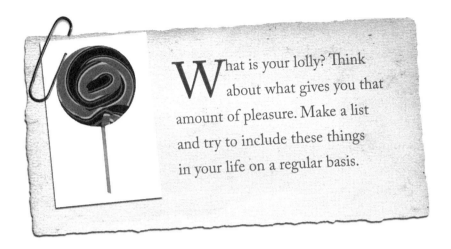

What is your lolly? Think about what gives you that amount of pleasure. Make a list and try to include these things in your life on a regular basis.

I gave another boy a lolly, and then his little sister came running up moments later. As she approached I started to unpack my backpack again to reach for another sweet. Before I even had a chance to open it, he looked at me and smiled. I thought 'Here we go, I'm going to get asked for another lolly'. But I wasn't. Instead he got his lolly, bit it in half, and gave half to his sister.

She was about three and he was maybe five. They both looked at me and smiled. I just looked at them with tears in my eyes, puzzled as to why these people could be so happy when they clearly had so little. They couldn't imagine a world where a young woman traveller might have enough lollies to give one to each child.

Another moment that had a profound impact on me was when a young boy invited me to his family home without first asking his parents. They welcomed me in, using hand signals to ask me to sit. I noticed all they had to eat was boiled rice cooked in water with a pinch of salt. When the boy invited me in, his mother, rather than being angry at her child, just reached out and took a fifth from each of the plates of the five people in the small home, making me my own plate of rice. She added water and salt. The boy smiled at me, his new friend.

I just didn't get it. I walked out of the hut sobbing, trying to work out why these people were so happy and generous. They didn't seem to have anything, they seemed so poor and yet so rich and in high spirits. They smiled so much, they had beautiful skin – it was as if something inside of them just shone.

I don't know what happened to me on that trip but it was a major turning point for me. I remember sitting down and thinking, '*I want what they have*'.

And for someone who had been trained to show no emotions, it was a relief to just be me; to be able to express what I felt without judgment; to release stress that had been sitting under the surface for so long.

I came back from the trip to Nepal very confused, needing clarity about what I had felt and how to deal with it. My first call was to one of my mentors. I asked him to help me make some changes in life but told him I wasn't sure where to start. One of the things he recommended was to read inspirational books. Again, I didn't know where to start, so I decided to send an email to people I considered well-read, asking them what they'd read that they had found inspirational.

> *… read as much as possible. Read about inspiring people in business, autobiographies, read about people in similar situations. For me one that hit me was Anyone Can Do It by Bobby and Sahar Hashimi who started the Coffee Republic [chain] in the UK. – Abbie Martin*

By the time I compiled my list of must-read inspirational titles, I had thirty books. When I go, I go at a million miles per hour so I went and bought all thirty of them and ordered the ones that weren't in the store. The bill was over a thousand dollars!

I don't know what happened to me on that trip but it was a major turning point for me. I remember sitting down and thinking, *'I want what they have'*.

Then I started to churn through them, one by one. I began to see a pattern in them, linking one concept to another, also noting the variants, and highlighting interesting passages as I read.

One book that had an enormous impact on me was by Stephen Covey, *The Seven Habits of Highly Effective People*. In the book, Covey describes a number of models that 'rang home' to me. Covey asked many questions including what you wanted to be remembered for. This got me questioning what legacy I wanted to leave behind. So I began to invent my funeral plan.

First I was perplexed. I was completely stuck; I had no idea what my answer might be. Then I started to get really excited. I realised that I could create an image of what I wanted my funeral to look like and so I went about mapping it out.

When I started to map out my funeral, I realised I would like 1500 people at my funeral. I can honestly say there is a little bit of ego involved in that … but what it boils down to is this. I want to be able to say that when I die, 1500 people have been influenced or in some way affected through an interaction with me, either through one-on-one work that I've done with them, or because they've come to a workshop, or to hear me speak. Or perhaps they've been related to family or friends. These people would be affected enough for them to want to keep a relationship with me during their lifetime and then to come and celebrate my life at my funeral. I want to help change people's lives. I want to help people believe in themselves more.

And funnily enough thinking about my funeral led to a bigger life plan. It made me realise that I wanted to do more work with women and kids and with a large number of different organisations. I wanted to do charity work and I wanted to be a positive influence on people and the way they think. I wanted to challenge, to be blunt, and help facilitate growth.

It was just so liberating to find out what I really wanted to do and create an exciting concept like that.

So I now have a funeral plan, down to a seating plan. The fact that I'm a big foodie is built into my will so that costs can be allocated to it, and I'm going to leave very clear instructions about how I want my life to be celebrated. I want people crying at that funeral; I want people weeping like there is no tomorrow, feeling so sad that I've left the planet. That's the impact that I want to have! Egomaniac, yes. But hopefully doing some good in the process.

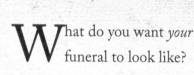

What do you want *your* funeral to look like?

Have a go. Lean back, close your eyes and then think what you would like your funeral to look like.

Who would you like to speak about you?

What would you like them to say?

Write your thoughts down.

This exercise gives us great insight into our values, and helps to clarify what is really important to us. Designing your funeral can be a great first step in defining your vision.

During this process I realised that the senior management roles in the corporate world that I had been working in – and working towards all my life – weren't going to fulfil this new dream I had.

> I was essentially overseeing the state government's books. The reason I left was that I always had a sense that there was something better for me, I wasn't sure what it was but I felt there was more out there for me. – Mark Priadko

> The risks were really big. It was hard leaving a corporate media job, with all the security of income and comforts of the environment I was surrounded by. I lost my networks and peers also. – Simone Preston

> When I look back now, leaving the security of my job with the uni was quite a risk, but more so in hindsight. Leaving that pay cheque, super, sick leave and those benefits was a really big thing. – Jennie Groom

Have you ever asked yourself 'who am I?', or felt dissatisfied with where your life is at? That dissatisfaction may be coming from your personal relationships, or from your professional environment. You need to go back and ask yourself:

> What exactly am I dissatisfied with?
> What exactly am I not feeling content with?
> What does it mean to be content?

It's something we spend our lives striving for when it is quite easy to find. For me, two moments stand out, two times in my life that I felt complete contentment. One was in my childhood and the other towards the end of the trip in Nepal. I had an incredible feeling of peace in Nepal. I felt clear that I had enough and did not need or desire anything else. I was not worried about anything in the past or the future, and I was just content to enjoy the present moment.

Go back to a time when you felt really content and look at the feelings you felt at that time. Think about the environment you were in. How can you recreate those feelings in your personal life and your business in the present?

My belief is that contentment comes with a feeling that you just have to be you, and when you are following your vision. You are in a place where you're being true to yourself. Your direction, your vision, your passions, are all heading in the same direction. Sometimes you think you're on the path doing the right thing but if you look at yourself, really dig deep into your feelings, you may admit that you're not content. And if you're not content, you're probably either not aware of your vision or not in alignment with your vision.

If you are looking at starting up your own business and haven't started that journey, or if you have started that journey and are still feeling dissatisfied, ask yourself the following questions:

What do I get passionate about?

Am I working in an area that is meeting my passion?

If not, what steps can I take to ensure I start to move towards my passion?

At any time if you are feeling dispassionate about your work, ask yourself:

Am I in alignment with the vision of my passion?'

If you are not in alignment with your higher purpose, it gets very difficult to keep your energy levels up and to feel passionate about what you're doing.

Many wise things have been said about having a vision:

The only limit to our realization of tomorrow will be our doubts of today. – Franklin D. Roosevelt

The great thing in this world is not so much where we are, but in what direction we are moving. – Oliver Wendell Holmes

And just remember: the ultimate source is within yourself. – Dalai Lama

Every time you don't follow your inner guidance, you feel a loss of energy, loss of power, a sense of spiritual deadness. – Shakti Gawain

Although I had my doubts and fears like most people who want to start up their own business, I knew deep within my soul that I had to do it. If I didn't, I might live to regret it – and life is too short to live with regrets.

Was I scared? Absolutely! I remember wondering whether this was an early midlife crisis. Probably I'd regret this later on. And although I felt fear, part of me was yearning to go and try this new thing out.

I was very clear on how I wanted to operate. I came up with a charter:
- Mutual respect – openness and diversity of ideas
- Integrity – doing what you promise
- Uniqueness – provide unique ideas and solutions
- Focus on relationships and outcomes – have a long term outlook.

Self-esteem was a real challenge in the beginning. – Jennie Groom

The toughest thing was the constant worry of not having enough money. That can really get you down a bit so that you start making decisions based on your bank account rather than what is best for your business. Your self-belief can be knocked about a bit if you are constantly focused on your finances. – Abbie Martin

I was worried about money. From earning a large sum of money and having the security of a job, I was not sure if would have enough money for my basic needs. I looked at how much money I would need if I went into starting my own business. I included a night out a week, a short holiday once a year and rent. The overall yearly budget was approximately

$34,000 and I decided to give myself two years to make this work. If it did not work by the end of the two years, I would find another job. I knew it would be for much less money than I was used to, but it would be okay if my risk did not pay off.

> *My biggest risk has really been my book because of the amount of money I have invested in it. – Jennie Groom*

> *I kept the financial risk low by minimising overheads and by being aware of income stream. – Katrina Webb*

I thought it would be worthwhile to meet up with different people who had already been running their own business successfully. I wanted to chat, get advice, and get energised. In the end I found that this process had a life of its own. I started off ringing some people I knew, who told me about *other* people they knew, who then told me about *other* people they knew, till I got hold of the right people. All of these wonderful people started to come into my life, and I had so many fascinating interactions and heard so many stories of successes and failures.

I wanted to talk to people as I thought it might help me further understand who I really was and how to achieve what I really wanted to do. My process was to ring someone up and say 'Your name's been given to me by xyz and they said that you were a leader in the field of abc business. I know you don't know me from a bar of soap but I would so appreciate twenty minutes of your time. I would love to tap into your brain and run some things by you and see what you think before I make this very big transition into starting up my own business. Can I buy you a coffee at a time that suits your diary?'

> *I believe in continually reinventing yourself, and I do this in my products and pricing. – Janelle Gerrard*

I rang twenty-four people and only two people said no: one who was involved in a project with a very tight timeframe, and the other was overseas. I was amazed that these very busy and successful people would willingly give their time to someone they didn't even know. And I will be forever grateful to them for that.

One woman, Kate, was just extraordinary. She had been running her business for more than fifteen years. One day I was sitting at a café waiting for her and she was running late. It was ten minutes past the time we were supposed to catch up, and my fear started to rise. I thought 'Perhaps she's not going to show up … Perhaps this is going to be one person who doesn't have time for me'.

She arrived late, sat down and apologised profusely for her delay. She went on to share with me the most extraordinary work she and her team were doing both in Australia and overseas on management of boards. As I listened to her, I realised there was a commonality between her and the other people I had met. She was willing to share the knowledge she'd gained from fifteen years in her business, but also the wisdom she'd gained in all of her life. She was willing to share this with me just to give me a head start. I could not believe that somebody would just distil all their knowledge and wisdom and give it to me in a package that felt like a present!

I had initially asked Kate for twenty minutes to half an hour of her time. Two hours later our two coffees had turned into dinner and a bottle of wine. In the end, I was with Kate for over five hours. And in those five hours the wisdom that she shared with me saved me months of work.

What amazed me even more was that Kate wasn't unique among these people. The willingness to help was astounding from them all.

Ask people for help and their expertise. Hardly anyone says no!
A couple of useful things to mention are:

Let them know how you found out about them.

Acknowledge them for their success before asking for anything else. They have worked hard and smart to be successful and deserve praise.

Be clear about which areas of their expertise you want to 'tap' into, ie marketing, finance, or customer relationships.

Explain your situation and that you will have questions for them (you can send these to them in advance if they request it) so they know that you have done your homework.

People I met through my continued efforts at networking were very generous with their support. – Janelle Gerrard

From my experience with these twenty-two meetings, I learnt the importance of just asking people for help. Invite them into your life, be open about asking for help, and treat them with honour and respect as you tap into their wisdom.

Essentially, you are saying to these people: 'I would like to tap into some of your wisdom and talk to you about some of the ups and downs of running your own business. I would like to know about your vision, about what you wanted to create and how you did it.'

People will give you their time and wisdom because they feel flattered. And, in fact, often you'll find that someone helped them when they started.

Their input is so helpful because it's completely independent. It's from somebody who has an external perspective, who doesn't know you, and isn't so close to you that their vision can be clouded.

People like this can provide you with blunt answers to your questions. Secondly, quite simply, their experience is different to yours, especially if you are just starting out. Tapping into the knowledge of people who have 'been there and done it' results in extraordinarily quick learning.

When I think back I am amazed at what I learnt in that short period.

I learnt the importance of just asking people for help. Invite them into your life, be open about asking for help, and treat them with honour and respect as you tap into their wisdom.

Eventually it was time to make my move. It was time to walk into my boss's office, this person who'd been so supportive of my journey and had offered me so many opportunities, and share with him my decision. I dreaded letting him down. I had to tell him that not only was I going to refuse the next natural step in my career, which we'd discussed before my trip, but that I was going to leave!

The gap in the market I found was consulting and coaching. There were many people working in these areas providing results that were expensive and slow in delivery. I wanted to be able to provide the client with immediate, short-term results for a better price. I knew I could help people grow themselves and their businesses by asking them more direct questions, identifying their needs faster than others, and delivering solutions to meet their needs.

As I had hoped, my boss responded to the news well and was very encouraging of my new adventure. Although the organisation was going through a lot of change and my current role was about to change significantly, he was very gracious about the time I'd picked to leave. I was so grateful that my desires were seen as positive, something that I wanted to create for myself, rather than being viewed in a negative light.

Then it was time to sit down with my family. It was very intense sitting there and telling them that I was leaving my secure job, starting up my own business. As I shared my vision with them, I remember seeing excitement coupled with worry and fear in their eyes. It was hard not taking that fear on – because I was so worried about letting them down as well as letting myself down.

I had grown up with wonderful family support and now I was going to go against the grain of what I had been taught and let go of everything I'd built up in my life from a material perspective. Not only that, but I was letting go of the very large sum of money that I was earning. Instead

I was heading off into the unknown to manifest this dream which was exciting and stirring me at a deep level even though I did not yet quite know how to make it work.

My mum asked me in her beautiful Indian accent, 'Shivani, are you sure this is what you want to do?'

I looked into her eyes and I replied 'Mum, I am not 100 per cent sure but I'm never going to know until I give it a try'.

As I drove home from my parents' place, I felt unsure of myself and this decision I'd taken. Was it too late to go back to my boss and reverse my decision?

I had my business idea – but I had very little actual knowledge about how to set it up and what needed to be done. I spoke to various people who I had met recently who had started up their own business and asked them how they were going about learning. They passed on a couple of government websites which I was able to download some business plans from. But as I was unclear of what I wanted, it was very confusing to know exactly where to start and what to do – what actual form my business should take.

I knew I could do many things.

- Should I be an expert in one or two areas or become more of a generalist?
- I knew what range of pricing to charge from interviewing others, but was I better off having low margins and a high volume of business or high margins and a low volume?
- Should I collaborate with other people on projects or should I do them by myself?

I knew what my strengths were, but my weaknesses were untested. My strengths included:

- coming up with creative ideas;

Once you're working in an area of your passion, then it does not feel like hard work. It no longer feels like one long round of *oh my God I have to achieve these targets and I've got so much to do here and so much to do there …* instead, it feels natural.

- finding solutions to difficult problems;
- getting people to open up about challenges they were facing.

My weaknesses included:

- managing invoices;
- book-keeping;
- and knowing which systems to use when setting up in the business.

Part of me said 'Maybe I should just stick to the parts that I'm really good at'. The other part of me said 'Maybe I should just do the bits I enjoy', knowing that it was the bits I hadn't been enjoying in my job that had led me down this path in the first place.

In the end my fear got the better of me. In hindsight I can see that in the first three years, I ended up doing a lot more of what I was good at which included consulting, and only slowly started to make the transition into doing more of what I loved, which was more coaching and transformational leadership work. After the first three years, I focused on areas of passion and learnt skills when I needed them.

Once you're working in an area of your passion, then it does not feel like hard work. It no longer feels like one long round of *oh my God I have to achieve these targets and I've got so much to do here and so much to do there* … instead, it feels natural.

We care about outcomes, genuinely – which means we do the little things and take care of the details. – Katrina Finlayson

Do something that you love, then you will never have to work another day in your life. – Julian Burton

Finding your higher purpose

So how *do* you go about finding out what your passion is? For me, it's a three-pronged process of working out your vision, your values, your principles. In one sense I worked it out the minute I decided to start the business – I knew that I wanted to work for myself, that I wanted to make a difference, that in particular I wanted to make a difference for women. But because of limiting beliefs that I may be seen as a feminist, and not being entirely clear what my vision was, it took me a couple of years to feel that I had a clear picture of the vision, values and principles for my business.

I found Maslow's hierarchy of needs a good way to start thinking about my vision, values and principles. Maslow's hierarchy of needs, as I understand it, explains what finding our higher purpose is about and what motivates us.

Maslow, a psychologist, studied a group of high achievers such as Albert Einstein and formulated a hierarchy of human needs which he grouped together (physiological, safety, love, and esteem). He suggested that each level of need must be satisfied before a person can act unselfishly. The lower-level needs are the basic necessities of life; towards the tip of the pyramid they become more to do with self-fulfilment. As long as we are motivated to satisfy these cravings, we are moving towards growth, toward self-actualisation.

Needs have an influence over our actions. A teenager may have a need to feel that he or she is accepted by a group; others of us are motivated by success or money. According to Maslow, when one of our needs is met, another, higher need emerges. Once these in turn are satisfied, again new (and still higher) needs emerge, and so on.

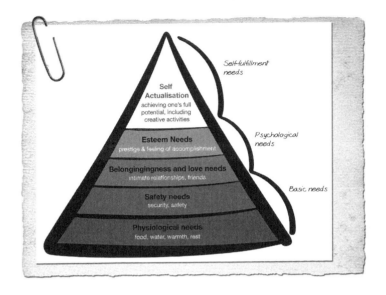

- Physiological needs are the basic needs such as air, water, food, sleep. When these are not satisfied we may feel sickness, irritation, pain, discomfort, etc.
- Shelter/safety needs are about creating stability and consistency. These needs are mostly psychological in nature. We need the security of a home and family.
- Social/love needs. Humans have a desire to belong to groups: clubs, work groups, religious groups, family, gangs, etc. We need to feel loved by others, to be accepted by others.
- Ego/esteem needs. This kind of need is to do with the recognition that comes from others. 'Look what I can afford!' Naturally the healthiest esteem is the one that comes from within, knowing that you are good enough, clever enough, and lovable enough.

- Self-actualisation needs are needs for a higher purpose. Seeking alignment in your life is part of this. Once all other needs are satisfied, we reach this stage. At this point we typically ask questions like: 'Am I really happy? What would make me happy? What is important to me? What legacy do I want to leave behind?'

I felt that this model applied to me in the following ways:

I – unlike many people in third world countries who live on or below the poverty line – don't have to worry about food, water or shelter (physiological and safety).

I belonged to many social groups – sporting, friends, family, cultural and networking.

Since the age of fourteen, I had spent most of my time on my need to achieve, to get further, to earn more money, to drive the right car, to live in the right house, and had felt dissatisfied despite achieving these goals (ego).

When I got to Nepal, my other needs had been satisfied and I was questioning my higher purpose or my passion. I felt at peace at some level knowing I had been put on this planet to achieve a higher purpose (self-actualisation).

Why not apply Maslow's hierarchy of needs to your own life? Have a look at where you have been in the past and where you are now.

> Today my vision is to inspire, challenge and transform a billion people to believe in themselves. – Shivani

Find your vision

Visions can change. When I first had the vision for my business, I just wanted to help people grow. My vision has evolved as I have evolved.

When you're formulating a vision, be grand about it. Don't think small, think BIG. The wonderful thing about business is that you can have a global vision but still operate on a state, local or even a regional level, depending on where you are in your business.

> *The mind is the limit. As long as the mind can envision the fact that you can do something, you can do it – as long as you really believe 100 per cent. – Arnold Schwarzenegger*

Imagine who is buying or using your product or services.

Are you operating at a local or international level?

Which is the best market to help you realise your vision?

What are your values?

A value is a framework you operate from. Defining your values is about setting up a framework from which you will operate.

Starting a business starts with you. What do you want your life to be? How does the business fit in? Do you want to run an empire? Do you want to set up a business that allows you to just work fifteen hours a week? Do you want to have much flexibility? Do you want to have as many happy customers as possible? It is difficult to decide how you want your business to be prior to making some decisions around how you want your life to be – as your business naturally will have a large impact on your life.

So if you have thought about your vision – where you want your business to be heading, defined what you are naturally good at and how you would like the business to fit into your life, it is time to define the values of your business.

I have worked with many managers and leaders who have struggled with individuals who are technically brilliant but are causing issues in the workplace. I believe that unless the person working in the organisation has the same set of values as the organisation itself, there is misalignment which will come across in the form of issues. I have advised many HR practitioners that they could think about hiring based on values and that individuals could also put their values in their CVs to help HR and in the interview process.

> *If we adhere to values we have in our minds, our responses and reactions will be based in values not just our quick ego reaction.*
> *– Eleanor Roosevelt*

Finding your values

What do you really admire in a friend?

List at least five attributes, without thinking too much.

The attributes we value in a friend are the things we value in ourselves. Use this list as a starting point for coming up with a list of your own values.

What are your principles?

Many teachers believe there are universal principles that we should all follow if we want good quality of life. These are:

- How we treat others.
- How we operate (this is similar to the charter I mentioned earlier).
- Making a difference – whether this is for a local charity or helping in the school canteen.
- Taking pride in everything we do.
- Continuing to learn and grow ourselves before attempting to do it for others.

It is difficult to decide how you want your business to be prior to making some decisions around how you want your life to be – as your business naturally will have a large impact on your life.

It's been like an apprenticeship in learning how I can maximise my influence and effect on change in sustainability and in the corporate world. In the last two years I have done a lot of work with corporations, governments and groups such as the United Nations. We essentially go to corporations and advise them on how they can achieve a competitive advantage through sustainable practice, and responsibility toward issues like climate change, because people forget easily how important the climate really is to just about every industry. Our response is so linked to the future of our businesses and the survival of these corporations and essential industries. – Nick Palousis

Working with your vision, values and principles

Once we have defined our vision, values and principles, we need to adhere to them in our business and private lives. We need to work 'inside out', starting with our character and motives; this naturally is an ongoing process. We know from experience that if we want to improve relationships with others, we must improve the relationship with self first.

In a relationship, for example, if you work from the outside in, you might feel victimised and immobilised, perhaps you'll focus on the weaknesses of other people and the circumstances responsible for your situation. Probably our first instinct is to focus on wanting to *change* our spouse or business partner.

Ultimately the 'outside in' approach never lasts. Many studies show that most lottery winners tend to revert back to how they felt before the initial high. Or as we all know … going shopping feels good when we get the new purchase home, but very quickly that feeling is gone.

We have these kinds of recurring issues in our private lives – but also in business. The question is why? Recurring issues are a way for us to learn to deal with things. They are there to teach us a lesson. For example, we often focus on outcomes rather than people. This may lead to unnecessary clashes, and to achieve our goals we will have to learn to deal well with people. Or it could be that we repeatedly experience running out of money from pay to pay, or that we get into situations where we feel taken for granted and used. Rather than blame the outside world, try to see your pattern in these events. It is so much easier seeing everybody else's 'stuff', but that's not to say that you should give up trying to see yours more clearly.

> *You have got to be authentic, remain true to yourself because there is no greater satisfaction than doing this. Surround yourself with good people, people you can trust, people that are honest; this is critical. Remember you have to have the fierce conversations, I'm really big on this. I mean the right conversations, with the right people at the right time. Get a handle on this and it will really make a difference. Finally to sum up, you always have to be grateful for what you've got, and always have the attitude that you can give. – Julian Burton*

We tend to be 90 per cent occupied with what we can observe: 'Oops, I need to get some more milk; What do I look like? My trousers feel tight – have I put on weight? I wonder if he/she likes me? I don't like her'. Being proactive is more than taking initiative; it involves taking responsibility (*response-ability*, or our ability to respond) for our lives.

Our behaviour is a function of our decisions, not our conditions.

When we are highly *proactive* we do not blame circumstances, conditions or conditioning for our behaviour.

When we are highly *reactive* we are very sensitive to factors out of our control such as the weather, the moods of others, traffic etc.

Are you reactive or proactive? Test yourself through your language:

My work was very engaging, working closely with important people, but a sense of purpose inside of me took me on a different journey. —
Mark Priadko

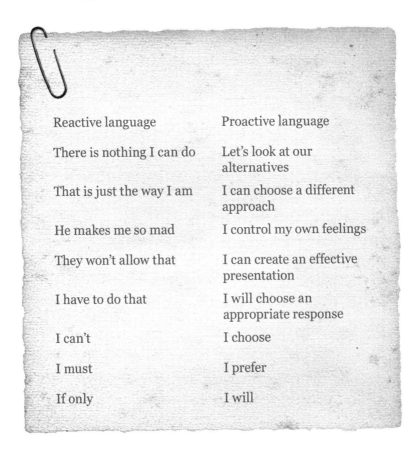

Reactive language	Proactive language
There is nothing I can do	Let's look at our alternatives
That is just the way I am	I can choose a different approach
He makes me so mad	I control my own feelings
They won't allow that	I can create an effective presentation
I have to do that	I will choose an appropriate response
I can't	I choose
I must	I prefer
If only	I will

Try this exercise to see if you can find any non-alignments between your vision, values and principles.

Make a list of your most important goals (economic, professional, political, physical, spiritual, relational, family, artistic, national etc).

Can you find inconsistencies between them?

Which purposes do you have that you are aware of?

Which of them would you be unwilling to admit to?

Questions to ask around a specific purpose:

What exactly is my purpose in this situation?

What am I trying to accomplish?

What is the first thing I need to do to accomplish my purpose?

How does my purpose differ from that of my partner, peers or other managers?

Does my stated agenda differ from the actual one? If the answer is yes, would I admit to my actual one? If not, why not?

I was doing a public speaking course as I had had a speech impediment growing up. Simultaneously I was doing quite a bit of media work with various radio stations. And I reached this point where I realised if I'm going to make a go of this, whether that be the Burns Trust or the public speaking, that I will have to give it 100 per cent.
– Julian Burton

The inspiration of others

As part of this book, I interviewed business owners running a diverse range of businesses. Throughout the book you'll read quotes from those inspiring people, and their details are found in the Appendix.

My interviewees are enjoying success in their businesses and they all mentioned that the best kinds of business starts with you doing something you enjoy and are good at.

Chapter 2

Year 1: first lessons

Business name and logo ❧ Charging what you are worth ❧ Sense of isolation ❧ Finding my feet and redefining ❧ Dealing practically with fears ❧ Awards ❧ Set-up costs

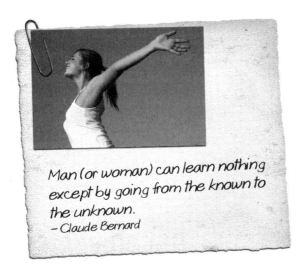

Man (or woman) can learn nothing except by going from the known to the unknown.
– Claude Bernard

Lesson 1: the power of feedback

When you begin a business, it's such an exciting time. You start to dream up a few business names and logos. I wanted to have a business name that told people what I did, and so I came up with *Reiter Business Consulting*. Reiter was my surname at the time, and I wanted people to know that my business worked with other businesses and that I was a consultant. Later I changed *Reiter* to *Real* so it was clear what my values were, what I stood for – and 'real' sounded simpler than 'authentic'.

I remember many people telling me not to use the word 'consulting'. It's the dirty 'C' word. Consulting has a lot of negative connotations, people said, and government departments wouldn't want to use my services.

But I thought: if that's what I do, then that's what I'll have in my business name. There is no point coming up with a trendy name that means nothing to me. At the time there were many businesses coming up with one-word company names which had no relation to what that business did, and that just didn't seem real to me.

But I thought: if that's what I do, then that's what I'll have in my business name. There is no point coming up with a trendy name that means nothing to me.

I believe your business name is a great marketing tool so use it wisely.

With my marketing background, I got very excited about my logo. Part of my research including looking at other people's logos and I brainstormed about fifty different ideas.

My favourite logo was based on a story I had heard in high school. The story went 'if you put a frog in boiling water, the frog will jump out. However, if you put a frog in room-temperature water and slowly heat up the temperature, the frog will not realise it is getting hotter and will boil to death'. I wanted to prevent businesses from dying a slow death, and help them notice the incremental change in temperature. My role in business was to help organisations not be a boiling frog! Excited with this thought, I designed a logo of a gorgeous frog with a cross over it saying 'Don't be a frog that dies a slow death. Change.'

> *You need to be able to see big and small. Really to be able to see things in the broad perspective but also to cross all the Ts and dot every I. To go out on your own you need big thinking and small thinking.*
> *– Mark Priadko*

In business, I had learnt that you can get too close to certain decisions and lose your objectivity, so it's important to have your ideas tested. I decided to ask ten friends, family members and a couple of potential clients their view of the business name and logo. The results surprised me. What I learnt was that most people liked the business name. 'I think

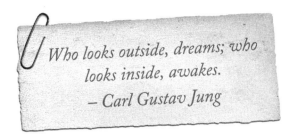

Who looks outside, dreams; who looks inside, awakes.
– Carl Gustav Jung

that's a great idea that you tell people what you're about and be clear on the type of consulting you will do' was a common response.

One of the great successes I've had has been the people I have involved in the trust, those that I am surrounded by essentially. They make all the difference, they can guide you and help you and at the end of the day it is the people that make an organisation. – Julian Burton

However the feedback that I got for the logo was that it was very complicated. I remember a conversation with my brother who said 'imagine you're at an event and handing out your card and explaining your logo. You've just spent two or three minutes trying to explain that particular story but you've lost them after thirty seconds! Why don't you make it really simple? Maybe you could use the story or imagery later on.' I don't think I was ready for that feedback because I was so hung up on that logo but as more people started to tell me that they had the same concerns with it, I needed to take that feedback on. In the end I came up with a very simple logo that used the letters RBC.

The lesson for me was testing the market and listening to the feedback. Feedback can bring you objectivity in an area that you may be too close to. Can you afford to test the whole marketplace when you're starting up a business? No! But asking a sample of the market, including people who love you and want you to succeed, and getting their constructive views, can really help.

My dad came up with an idea for a particular medical device and suggested I could carry it beyond the idea stage so I took it on, and built it up from there to where I was exporting to 44 countries before I sold it and moved into my current business. – Kea Dent

Feedback

What areas do you need feedback in?

Who will give you feedback in a nice but constructive manner?

Why don't you ask them?

And then reflect. If, like me, your gut reaction may be to ignore the feedback – do give it a bit of time. You might realise that the feedback is right. And, as my brother said, if you really love it, whether it's a logo or an idea, you can always come back to it later on.

Lesson 2: slow beginnings

I now had a brand new business name and logo, a brand new computer, a brand new mobile, a brand new telephone and an office set up with furniture so I could work from the back room of my house. I also had my new business cards printed with my new logo and business name. My business was registered and I was all ready to go!

I got to day one and realised that I had no customers. I had not created relationships and customers who would give me work before I walked out of my previous role. I had travelled extensively for my last job, and so most of my relationships were not based locally.

Being a positive person, the first morning, I made a list of what I wanted to do that day and what still needed to be done that week. The first day passed really slowly and I looked at the clock tens of times. Not one person rang me.

Day two, I was still really quite positive, not as much as day one, but day two was passing slowly as well and I got to the afternoon feeling a little bit down that nobody had rung me or contacted me. I was starting to worry how I was going to make any money. How would anyone know I was available?

It's an overall game overcoming self-doubt, you just have to chip away at that challenge all the time and stay true to your thoughts. Self-doubt is number one. I mean you have this inner belief that you can do it, but until you start to prove it to yourself you wonder: can you really?
– Julian Burton

My business will involve more overseas marketing and commitment and time, it is quite an emotional risk and has been already. Stepping out like that can affect your self-belief and I'm finding you really have to let go of the worry. Also the risk of leaving behind the athletic world, which makes up a big part of who I am is a risky thing in itself.
– Katrina Webb

Day three I remember vividly. By lunchtime, I finally broke down into tears. I started to have a lot of doubts and my little voice inside my head went 'Shivani, what have you done? You have left this senior, secure position with great money to go and start up this business and you know nobody and you have no clients. You are not going to survive!' I remember just bawling my eyes out at my desk.

Lesson 3: know what you're worth

On day four something very exciting happened. I received a call from John, one of the local managers at McDonald's. They were putting together a team-building day, they'd procured a facilitator, and now they wanted somebody to co-facilitate and manage some of the staff while they did their outdoor team activities. I was so excited. I knew the importance of the following question so I asked 'How did you find out about me?' John said that Wayne, someone I'd met recently, had recommended me. He knew I'd just started the business and had suggested me because he was very busy and couldn't take on the job himself.

Wow! Someone had recommended me already. The voice inside my head said 'You are going to be OK! You're good!' Not only was the first potential client on the phone, but it was McDonald's, one of the best business models around the world with over 18,000 outlets. I could see dollar signs spinning in my head!

There was the empty bookings book for a start. I had to find clients, and my target market and even a place to practise. I just tackled these challenges head on. I found a street with a health food shop on it and various other businesses that I thought would attract the sort of people that would be interested in my service. I also chose the area based on socio-economic factors. I actually convinced the owner of the health food shop that a small unused space at the back of his store would be a perfect place for me to use and he built a couple of walls and rented me the space. – Kylie Armstrong

So I asked John what would be involved in this role. I could tell that he was in a hurry and really just wanted to get off the phone. Then I asked the question that I felt really uncomfortable asking 'So … John, I was wondering what the pay would be for me to come and do this – and yes, I am available that day'. The team-building day was in two days' time.

John explained, 'We have a pretty tight budget. This is really a bit of an extra, and our budget is around $20 to $25 per person per hour'. A wave of disappointment washed over me and I got stuck with how to manage this, as the hourly and daily rates I'd decided to charge were much higher. 'John, would you mind if I gave you a call back within the next fifteen minutes?' I asked, and he replied, 'That would be fine'. I hung up.

I felt really confused. I wasn't sure whether I had done the right thing by not saying 'yes' straightaway. Naturally, I could see the benefits of having a company like McDonald's on my CV. But then I'd set my rates after lots of thought and research. Here was my first potential job – should

I really take it despite the money on offer?

I decided to ring an informal coach in the same industry and ask him for his opinion. He did what a good coach would, and asked, 'What do *you* think?'

I replied, 'I think that the money is too low'.

'Well, that's your answer,' he said. 'If you go into the marketplace at that rate, why would anyone else pay more later? It will be difficult to justify a higher rate later and you will confuse the marketplace. You have to be consistent. And are you a co-facilitator or are you a consultant and a facilitator? So you have to get those roles right, you have to get that clarity.'

> *I feel you should specialise in one thing. This way you can become the best at what you do and stand out from the crowd. – Kylie Armstrong*

I thanked him and put down the phone.

I dreaded making the call to John. I explained to him that my rate was much higher than they could offer me. Thankfully, he understood, and as I thanked him, I said 'If there's anything else I can do to help you in the future, please do let me know'. I remember feeling like I'd lost out.

I know the money was low. I didn't really need an affirmation of that and yet had sought it. When push came to shove, I'd been close to undervaluing myself. I had to become clearer about my motivations and expectations.

How much is too much?

Another question to ask yourself is: *how much is not enough?* If you have issues with charging, consider why this might be.

> *Do you think you are worth it?*
>
> *Do you feel that they would still like you if you charge your rates?*

What do you consider a fair price for your services? Compare
this with your competitors.

Lesson 4: don't be isolated

Another lesson I learnt in the first two weeks was that I really like being around people. Of course I knew I was an extrovert (Myers Briggs or MBTI had me profiled as an extreme E for extrovert. I scored 22 out of a possible 22!), but I'd never really been tested in this way before – I'd always worked in an office around people, or out of the office with clients. Suddenly, here I was in my back room of my house, alone. I felt very isolated in those first few months. I found that it was really important for me to feel like I was part of a business community. I have spoken with many others who have and continue to feel isolated.

> *Isolation, not having my team of people; that was tough. I had a good network of women in business so I used them to bounce ideas off and effectively redefined my team to people outside of work. Then there was the challenge of self-confidence and belief. Deep down I knew I could do it so I just kept pushing through it all with the help of my support network. I believe you just have to challenge and keep pushing yourself.*
> *– Jenny Carmuciano*

This was the most common issue mentioned when businesspeople were interviewed around Australia for this book. I asked them what was tough for them when they first started out in business. Most felt lonely, isolated and really missed being around people. One mentions how she missed not getting dressed for work, not having anyone to bounce ideas off. She dealt with it through choosing to work within the office of the clients she was working for at the time. Another one mentioned that he missed little things like cold drinking water in the office, he also found it a challenge to be his own IT expert, for instance. Self-motivation is also mentioned by many. It is easier to propel downwards when you're not surrounded by others – even if it is as simple as having someone else to act as a sounding board.

> *Motivating myself has been tough, but that isn't so much due to the isolation of working on your own, it's probably more closely related to at times having too much freedom. I mean the office relationships are really work relationships, they lubricate the work experience, like a little chit chat on a Monday morning, but these are those luxury aspects that you learn to live without. – Mark Priadko*

> *I am also in the process of creating a peer network to connect people doing this type of work, basically to recoup some of those environmental and support losses we've talked about. Nikki Seymour-Smith*

Are you finding your business isolating? You're not alone. The answer is to find ways of being with other like-minded people. Think about these ideas:

> *sharing an office space*
>
> *networking regularly with others in a similar line of work*
>
> *meeting clients for coffee*

Let me share the story of Kate, a coaching client. Kate had decided that she wanted to leave the corporate world and start running her own business. She excelled in technical documentation work, particularly in the area of occupational health and safety, and had the ability to transform complex problems into simple solutions. Some of her work involved face-to-face meetings with the client to determine their needs; however, most of her work was sitting in a spare room in her house, doing the documentation work on her computer.

Within three or four months of starting her own business, Kate was craving contact with other people. Despite the business providing her flexibility in hours, the freedom of being her own boss, and good revenue and cash flow, she felt isolated.

Having experienced this myself, my coaching work with Kate focused on developing appropriate networks and also helping to boost her self-confidence when it came to approaching people. In business, it is so important to be with like-minded people, even if you don't actually share an office with them. Humans are social beings, and the stimulation of others' company can be a great business tool, as much as anything else.

John Gray, author of *Men are from Mars, Women are from Venus*, a worldwide best-selling book, spends regular time with like-minded people. He regularly gets together with friends like Jack Canfield, author of the bestselling *Chicken Soup for the Soul* series, and they share ideas and concepts.

> *Feeling alone and totally out on a limb was new to me, I had been so used to the group environment surrounded by easily accessible feedback and support, as well as inspiration and energy. There were two keys to dealing with this.*

> *The internet was invaluable, and small business networks and courses with like-minded people gave me a source of peers. The other key was discipline, every day in that first year when I was working out of home I would dress up for the office like a normal workday even though I was going to another room in the house. – Janelle Gerrard*

> *Self-esteem was a real challenge in the beginning. Being worried about the image I was projecting professionally, you know, driving a kombi, working from home and not being able to bring people to my office. – Jennie Groom*

Lesson 5: use your contacts

Although I'd had the initial buzz of the phone call from McDonald's, it wasn't enough. I knew that I was going to have to get out there and be proactive if I really wanted to make this a success.

So I decided I could no longer wait for clients to come to me. I know it sounds very simple in theory but it's much harder in practice. Suddenly you're selling yourself. Even if you've worked for companies where you essentially had to sell yourself, you're still doing it under the banner of someone else's company. Marketing yourself and your business is another thing entirely.

Before beginning the business, I'd allowed myself to think that I was going to have people knocking at my door as soon as they knew I was up and running. Of course, by now I'd realised how wrong I was! This is just not how start-up businesses of my kind worked.

I needed to go and 'press flesh' – network!

My first step was to go and talk to my old boss. Starting with someone I already had a relationship with seemed sensible. I could talk to him about what I was doing in more detail, and find out about any opportunities I could help with.

A rule of thumb in business is that it costs four times more to procure a new client than to work with an existing one.

Within an hour of ringing my old boss and leaving a message, he'd rung back to arrange a meeting. I was in his office the next day. He asked me to run customer satisfaction surveys, which they had previously outsourced. He wanted to utilise my experience to 'in house' them. All of a sudden, in week two, I had just won my first job! That was fantastic because I really needed some encouragement after a few tough days.

When I first started there was nothing, I thought it was an absolute picnic, because I had work, and quite a lot of it, come straight to me. I seem to have never really had to send out asking for work since my first few emails that brought me in two specific lines of work, and from there word of mouth plus my performance have really carried the business through. – Mark Priadko

> *Make a list of who you know and have an existing relationship with both personally and professionally. Let these people know that you are now running your own business. It's much easier than cold-calling people you don't know and you're far more likely to succeed.*
>
> *Studies suggest that while around 5 per cent of cold calls are successful, that number leaps to 15 per cent when a call is made as a result of a referral. If a phone call or email has been made on your behalf, then 50 per cent of the time you're likely to get the green light.*

This job was a six-week project for three days a week – and a fantastic start. It also made me feel that I'd left the company on a good note. It was great to be hired back straight away, and I felt really valued. I felt indebted to my old boss and the organisation for allowing me the opportunity to do project work with them.

As the project progressed, I realised I was back in my comfort zone. I no longer had my swanky office and instead was in the 'consultants' corner'. The people who'd previously been my colleagues would come and talk to me, and at times I felt as if I had never left.

The major difference was that I wasn't part of the leadership team anymore, and found it difficult to continue conversations not knowing all of the information. I noticed that a few people came up and whinged about internal politics, telling me all the things that were wrong and some of the things that weren't working for them. I realised the same people had whinged in my office previously. The difference was, I didn't have to take on any issues this time round, so I communicated that message and received some shocked looks.

As the project progressed, I realised that getting back into the comfort zone was not what I'd set up my own business for. I needed to take more risks. At the end of that six-week project, I made a decision not to work more than two days a week with any one customer. I did not want a handful of clients. Instead, I wanted to be able to get as much experience and diversity as possible from a marketing and experience perspective, which meant having a good and broad range of clients. I knew this would mean that there might be days where I'd have nothing to do – but it was in alignment with my vision to work with hundreds of companies and influence a diverse range of people.

Lesson 6: make free days creative days

One of the informal mentors I met gave me a brilliant idea. He told me, 'The best thing in business is when you have a day where you have nothing to do. How fantastic – because it means that you can look at creating something for yourself that day. Why not start putting workshops together, questionnaires, or ideas for new products?' And the list went on. Rather than looking at a day without client work as a missed opportunity, use it to generate more business.

> *Motivation was a challenge too, just being so free with your time. I really had to work at that by committing to exhibitions, doing a bit of deadline creation and finding projects like my book. Areas I was passionate about came easily. – Jennie Groom*

> *Discipline has really helped me. Discipline in creating work/rest boundaries, mental discipline in staying committed and continually evolving and pushing myself to change through engagement of other people. – Janelle Gerrard*

Start a list of things you'd like to do, for example researching a particular topic. When you get that spare day, go back to that list and start actioning it.

I had been thinking of doing a particular workshop for a long time. I wanted to call it PacWomen! Let me explain why. When I was growing up I used to play a computer game called PacMan. There was a face with an open mouth that would go around eating pellets, and you had to eat as many pellets as you could in a very quick space of time. I remember wondering, *why can't women eat pellets?* Why is it called PacMan? Why isn't it called PacWoman?

My idea with my 'creative' days initially was to think about this workshop idea properly. I began by thinking about my own past work experience. Having worked in the very male-dominated engineering world, I looked at what I'd found hard to handle in that environment. I found it difficult to manage emotions in the workplace while keeping my credibility. I found it difficult to know the scale of assertively communicating my message – was I being a doormat, too passive, or was I being too aggressive in wanting to be heard?

I wanted to share the lack of work-life balance I'd felt while working in the corporate world with other women. I wanted to put together a workshop that captured these topics and more. In my first six months, I used many creative days to piece together the workshop for women which I ended up calling 'PacWomen' initially – now it's called Transformation for Business Leaders (although it's still aimed at women).

What amazed me during this process was how excited I was and how relatively easy I found the process – because it resonated with my passions! When I was doing project work at my old workplace, I found the work easy, and I was back in my comfort zone – but I was not enjoying it. I was doing it for the money. It was not challenging me. I wasn't growing in any particular way. It was only when I started to put together this workshop that I found myself smiling a lot despite not knowing how to market it and get the 'bums on seats'. But unlike the other work, it challenged me, it excited me. I knew this was the beginning of something that I needed to continue with – working with my passions.

I did a workshop called Women Leading Change. I was inspired by these powerful women at this course and the amazing and influential work they did, which to me and my definition of just making things look beautiful was quite intimidating and got me questioning myself.

Over those three days I came to realise that within myself I was actually unhappy in my life and I seriously needed change. So I did the course in August, and in November I sold the house. I took a sea change from Sydney to shake up every part of my life. – Janelle Gerrard

When you're working in an area of passion, ideas and solutions come easily, there is flow. When we force things, they do not flow and this is a signal that we are caught back in our ego. Our ego may want us to work in our comfort zone and tell us that we need money and that it is not safe to venture out living our purpose.

How do you feel when you do certain areas of your work? If it feels easy and flowing, it is a good indication that you are in alignment.

If the work feels difficult or is causing conflict, then it is not in alignment, and you can then take steps to not take similar work in the future.

Lesson 7: success breeds success

While I was transitioning into starting my own business, I had been nominated for the Telstra Businesswomen's Awards and I was absolutely startled. I didn't know why anybody would recommend me to go into any awards let alone a coveted business award that was very well-publicised. I felt the only reason I had been nominated was due to my past work and senior position. The person who nominated me had been a peer in the engineering world and felt that I handled things in that environment well. Fiona said to me, 'Shivani, I'm amazed at how much you've achieved at such a young age and I wanted to nominate you for these awards. I think you'd be a great role model!' Me – a role model … right! But I was touched by her comments. Looking at how I could fit in the very extensive submission process along with my current workload, I almost didn't want to go through the process. In the end the only reason I went ahead was because I did not want to let Fiona down.

What emerged out of this process was amazing. What I recognised was that when I started to go back into my life and into my history, there were many things I'd achieved that I'd forgotten about or buried so I would forget them. As I started to write some of these down, sometimes I thought they were so insignificant that the judges may feel the same: 'She *really* had to dig deep to get that little example!' but I decided to put them in anyway.

I focused on events which were turning points in my life, no matter what their impact on others had been. In my application, I discussed why I was so driven and determined and how I had achieved senior management positions at a young age. One of the awards I had won while studying engineering was the best student in the states of South Australia and the Northern Territory. I had been invited by the President of Engineers

What emerged out of this process was amazing. What I recognised was that when I started to go back into my life and into my history, there were many things I'd achieved that I'd forgotten about or buried so I would forget them.

Australia to receive this award and the story had been published in the local papers and various magazines. As my fellow students had dished out much 'crap' (a technical word!), suggesting that the Engineering faculty were just trying to encourage women to enter engineering, I felt embarrassed, and didn't look back at that event with any pleasure. Going through this process, I was able to finally enjoy that moment over a decade later.

Once the draft was ready, I emailed it through to my parents and to a couple of close friends, asking them for constructive criticism and feedback. I will never forget the phone-call one evening from my parents after they'd had the draft for a couple of days. Mum was on the phone. 'Shivani, this is fantastic that you've been nominated for the Telstra awards. I am so proud of you!' she said in her beautiful Indian accent, and then added, 'You have not mentioned in the document that you won Miss Whyalla.'

Miss Whyalla was a personality and beauty contest that I had won at the age of eighteen in the small country town of 28,000 people where I grew up. Mum reminded me how it made the *Whyalla News* and had caused quite a stir that somebody from another country had won it. A picture of me dressed as an Indian princess was on the front page. It was something that I copped a fair bit of criticism for at the time at school and like, the engineering award, I had buried it at the back of my mind.

I said 'Mum, I don't think that the judges are going to be that interested in me winning a Miss Whyalla award'. She thought for a moment and said, 'but Shivani, that was a turning point for you,' and I realised she was right. I had low self-esteem from racist comments that were made to me on a daily basis at school when I had moved to Australia at the age of eleven. Winning the award I was recognised as someone beautiful. Other women in Miss Whyalla that year were gorgeous young women, but I had won. I decided to add that to the submission and share that turning point.

Nervous attacks, bouts of doubting were quite fierce at first, especially with the suddenness of what I had done. Staying confident, positive and believing in myself was important. I just told myself I had to act quickly and decisively before I changed my mind. – Janelle Gerrard

I realised how important it was to work on a point of difference so that I stood out and so that on this I could develop the business. – Katrina Webb

Get family and friends involved in your nominations and success. This way, they get a chance – as do you – to reflect on your life, which is an award in itself. Not only that, but they might be able to add to your memories of your own successes.

I gave the submission 100 per cent, as I usually do in life, and I then let it go. I did not give it much thought once it was in. When I received a call several weeks later, I was completely surprised that I had been chosen as one of the six finalists in two categories. The next stage of the process was to have an interview with the judges.

I remember arriving at the interview nervously and then sharing my dream about having left the corporate world and starting up a small business. I convinced myself that the only reason the judges were impressed by me up to this point was because I had reached a senior position with a large corporation at a young age, and now that I had left, I had no chance. As I sat in the interview, though, I realised: *I'm a finalist.* I never expected to be nominated, let alone become a finalist, and I decided not to worry about the outcome and to stop questioning myself.

The day the winners were announced stands in my memory as if it happened yesterday. I walked into the Hilton where the awards ceremony was being held. It felt like I'd come to a ball although it was a lunchtime event. There were people buzzing around, excitement was in the air, inspirational music was playing and it felt like I had arrived at a mini-Oscars ceremony!

What took place over the next two and a half hours was transformational.

As each finalist was announced, faces were lit up onto two giant screens. I remember sitting at a large table with my family, friends and colleagues who had come to support me. When my face was on the screen hundreds of people were clapping. Looking at my parents, who were wolf-whistling, I had tears in my eyes. It was at that point I realised how much this process had been worth it, because I could see for myself how much support I had from my table of loved ones.

My father, who is fairly introverted, screamed my name and had tears in his eyes as I was announced the winner of the Young Businesswoman of the Year, for South Australia. They all continued to scream as did hundreds of others. A song was playing in the background, and I could hear the words 'heroes live for forever' as I walked up to the stage. I still get goosebumps when I relive that moment.

> *We forget how good we are. Other people look at us and go wow!*
>
> *We look at others and go wow! ... but how often do we go wow! at ourselves? Not enough.*

If someone nominates you for an award, please honour the person who has given you that opportunity and put your submission in. And most importantly, please honour yourself.

Marie Curie (1867–1934) was a remarkable woman, a physicist and the first woman to win a Nobel Prize – which she won twice – and the first woman to earn a doctorate in Europe. Her investigations led to the discovery of radioactivity as well as the element radium.

Ella Fitzgerald (1918–1996), is now considered one of the greatest jazz singers of all time. She was the winner of twelve Grammy Awards and awarded the Presidential Medal of Freedom.

Indira Gandhi (1917–1984), former prime minister of India, the world's most populous democracy. Indira Gandhi became an influential figure for Indian women as well as for others around the world.

Frida Kahlo (1907–1954), was a Mexican artist who survived childhood polio and later a bus accident that led to seven operations. She began painting to escape lifelong pain as a result of the accident and is considered one of the greatest artists of the twentieth century.

Margaret Thatcher (1925–present) was the first woman in European history to be elected leader of her country. Known for her conservative views, Margaret Thatcher was also the first British prime minister to win three consecutive terms in the twentieth century.

Later that year, I was also nominated for the Enterprising Women Awards and again I was fortunate enough to be the winner. The winnings did include money, but, more importantly, what came out of these awards for me were opportunities for further self-discovery.

This started me on the process of going back and looking at my vision to see if it was still what I wanted. And, importantly, it gave me the affirmation that people believe in me – sometimes more than I believe in myself.

Success brings more success and awards are a very cheap way of marketing yourself and your business.

At this stage I still followed the principle of not working for a client for more than two days per week. The awards did not bring direct work or business to me, but people associated with the awards started to market me as part of marketing the awards. So, by the end of my first year in business, I had conducted many two and a half day workshops and strategic planning meetings; and I'd run my first women's workshop. One of the major banks in Australia also suggested that I run a workshop for their clients, and this became the first step to developing what is now a workshop I run for businesses nationally.

Lesson 8: a good mentor is ...

There was a government-funded program offered that year called the South Australian Youth Entrepreneur Scheme (SAYES). It was offered to people under thirty, and they were provided with a mentor for a year. Those on the scheme were also granted free attendance at workshops on marketing, planning and so forth. The intake was limited and after undergoing an interviewing process, I was accepted.

This scheme allowed me, for the next twelve months, to work on my business plan, guided by industry experts. I also met a website designer through the program who ended up being the designer for my business for the next two years.

My mentor, who I was really excited about working with, worked in a law firm and was an entrepreneur himself. However; for the first three meetings he was more than half an hour late each time and the fourth meeting he forgot altogether!

When we come across people who are helping us, whether they're mentors or coaches, whether they're paid or unpaid, at the end of the day you are the client.

If someone providing you with a service is not meeting your needs, you are allowed to consider not continuing that relationship. This is not being ungracious but simply looking out for yourself. Bad help can slow you down more than no help.

You may find this hard, but be upfront about your needs and communicate them.

I remember feeling very frustrated, and wasn't sure how to handle the situation. I decided it was important to communicate this experience to the program director. I wanted to communicate that although my mentor was a nice guy and very experienced, I was finding him frustrating to work with, but I was very concerned about rocking the boat. On the other hand, I had many areas in business that I needed help with, and I needed someone reliable to bounce them off. I wanted a new mentor allocated to me, because I didn't want to waste this amazing opportunity by learning nothing. I was worried about pushing the friendship but I had little to lose. I spoke to the Director and explained my view and was allocated a new mentor. What I realised later on was that I had got my original mentor fired!

I met a fantastic man who became my manager. He looked after me in the sense of working out who I was and what I was about and he was really a great mentor in my life for about five years. Essentially he introduced me to my business, too.

As an athlete you only have a small window during which you can really compete so when you add up twelve years of thirty hours a week commitment and training you want to be able to draw from that beyond those experiences of competition. He opened me up to more deeply understanding and appreciating the athlete side of Katrina.
– Katrina Webb

When we come across people who are helping us, whether they're mentors or coaches, whether they're paid or unpaid, at the end of the day you are the client.

Here are some tips on what to look for in a mentor. You need someone who:

- *you can respect*
- *has accomplished things you admire and hope to achieve yourself. You need to be able to ask that person for guidance*
- *you can trust to be confidential*
- *is patient and has the time to spend going over your goals and working with you*
- *will be supportive, will encourage and challenge you and will motivate and inspire you to reach your full potential*
- *is genuinely interested in people and has a desire to help others*
- *knows how to effectively communicate, actively listen and give appropriate feedback*
- *is self-confident and does not see you as competition but rather appreciates a developing employee.*

And, if you're seeking your mentor from within an organisation that you work for, look for someone who takes pride in the organisation, relishes challenges and understands the vision and values of the organisation.

I get asked the question about mentors and coaches constantly – what is the difference? In my view, mentors are people that have experience in the areas you are discussing with them, such as a young lawyer being mentored by a more experienced partner in a law firm. A coach on the other hand does not have to have the same technical background but understands your industry, and asks you relevant questions that get you to clarify your thoughts and answer your own questions.

Lesson 9: you need to spend money to make money

Everyone told me you have to have a website. It makes communication with your clients easy but having never had one, I felt overwhelmed by the whole idea of it. Having an engineering degree, everyone expected me to 'get' technology ... which I found embarrassing on the occasions when, like with the idea of my own website, I didn't really 'get' the technology at all.

I also remember advice that was shared by a few people around me at the time: 'When you start a business, you've got to have long pockets and short arms' which basically meant don't overspend and be scarce with your money. I took this advice on board and set up a website using free space with my regular internet provider. The free website was difficult for customers to get into, people had problems spelling the address and therefore finding it, and it generally gave the impression I was a two-bit operator.

In retrospect, I was coming from a mentality of scarcity about money. If I had my time again, I would follow the philosophy that you have to spend money to make money and construct the website entirely differently.

That is not to say you give all your power to the web-developer. You still need to specify what you want the website to do. And you need to be able to measure your spend. For example, if a website cost $1000 and after a year you've ended up with twenty clients that you know have come to you through the website, and each of those clients have brought you approximately $500 worth of work – your website has paid for itself ten times over already in that first year.

On the other hand, one of my clients did not measure the spend on his website. He spent over $30,000 on it, and in the end had to discard it and start again. That is not wise.

Get involved in your website. Don't leave it at arms' length.

Monitor the cost but remember that spending money will make you money so think abundantly.

And ask questions. Don't worry about feeling or looking silly in front of others who may appear to be talking another language. Ask them to speak in a way you understand.

Chapter 3

Year 2: surviving hardship, growth and expansion

The effect of stories ❧ Balancing your personal life ❧
Emotional Intelligence and the value of relationships ❧
Networking ❧ Partnerships and other growth methods

The true mystery of the world is the visible, not the invisible.
– Oscar Wilde

The awards I won in my first year were a great experience, particularly the opportunity to meet so many high-achieving, focused women. It was the first time in my life that I felt I was in the company of like-minded women. I'd often had other women say to me, unprompted, 'Shivani, you're so driven, why do you need to achieve so much, why don't you just settle down, get married, have babies?' This felt like it was just a negative or defeatist outlook on life, and not one that I wanted to take on. Having been surrounded by males all my working life, though, I did occasionally wonder if these women were right. Was I too driven?

Lesson 1: it's not me, it's you

Meeting amazing women who were more driven than me was such a settling experience. One I particularly enjoyed meeting had won the National Telstra Business Woman of the Year Award a couple of years before me. Her name was Judith. She had nine children! She was studying an MBA. She ran a veterinary clinic. And she was very calming to be around. Well, she'd have to be! I remember thinking at the time: *nine kids and her own business, how does she do it?* So I asked her. She told me that she has help, and the kids all had tasks to complete each day. I was sitting there with her, talking with her about her experiences, and thinking to myself, 'I'm normal, I'm okay'. Gradually I began to realise that the negative feedback I'd been getting was maybe more about that person than it was about me. Perhaps they were not very happy about certain aspects of their life or needed to affirm choices they had made and wanted to project their views onto me.

One of the amazing things that came out of the awards was that I was requested to do more speaking. When you win an award people see you as an expert, and they want to put you in front of other people so you can share your experiences and your story. This got me in front of corporations including banks and recruitment companies who wanted me to share my story to inspire their staff. I also got to speak to young men and women in various schools and in front of a lot of women's groups. The exposure to these various businesses and groups was fantastic.

Many people I spoke to told me how amazing my story was. I found this hard to understand – I was just like them; my story felt ordinary to me. I had not really realised the impact of the awards at the time.

Slowly I began to see the future marketing implications of winning awards – not to mention the impact of the awards on my funeral plan (see page 7). I could see the possibility of actually achieving my dream of making a positive impact on the lives of many people. This allowed me to begin my funeral recruitment! I decided when speaking to share that story and vision and ask that if people had been inspired, to come and talk to me. That year, thirteen people joined the list to attend my funeral!

As I started to receive more requests for speaking, I wanted to improve my skills in this art. I went back to David, the speaking coach I had worked with when I was in the corporate world. I wanted to have more impact as a speaker which I found was very different to getting up and giving a corporate presentation. Among other things, I learnt breathing techniques and how to be more authentic. By authentic I mean when I was sharing a difficult experience like facing racism, I was still smiling. I was not feeling the emotion at the time. I learnt that I could feel being that eleven-year-old moving to Australia who had no friends and got made fun of. I could feel her anxiousness when she arrived at school and I did that each time I spoke, and began to come across more authentically.

I found that sharing my learnings and failures, rather than just focusing on my successes, was a more authentic way to present for me, and I received positive feedback from clients and audiences. I also was unsure of how much to charge so I ended up doing a speaker's business program for five days to get a better view of the bigger picture.

The program featured experienced and established speakers who shared their knowledge with the participants, and it was so useful. I learnt how to structure fees, and what to talk about, how to engage with the audience and much more.

Lesson 2: if you're not okay, don't pretend you are

Life balances itself. As many things were working in my business life, my personal life was the opposite. My marriage had started to reach crunch point. It hadn't been working from very early on but at this point I realised that it was not going to survive. I started to feel really stressed. Some people are able to differentiate between their personal and professional life by leaving one at the door. I am just not like that – and most people I have worked with also find it hard to separate out these things from one another.

I needed some help. I spoke to relationship counsellors, read books, talked to a personal coach. I knew the answer was to leave but felt like I had no guts to do it. And I was going insane with the pressure of maintaining the business with a smile while my marriage was going downhill.

My productivity started to reduce at work. I started to avoid my family and friends and not return their calls. My motivation for my business was at its lowest ever. 'What's the point? If I can't make my marriage succeed, what's the point of awards, what is the point of a successful business?' I remember saying to many friends and family members. Finally the marriage ended and so did a part of me. I had been so goal-oriented all my life, and this part of my life and the goals associated were now not going to be realised. I felt like a big failure. I'd failed my family, society and myself.

This was one of the darkest times in my life, and the decision to leave my marriage was the hardest one I've ever made. I felt really lonely and kept wondering if I had made a mistake. I oscillated between thinking, *is there any way it can work? can we try anything else?* to knowing we'd tried all these things for years and that there was no neat answer.

The relationship stakes were pretty high and I lost my husband in the process. Sometimes the test of support from your partner in following your dreams can be too much. – Simone Preston, Business Women Connect

Over a twelve-month period in my life I dealt with divorce, death and the challenge of new business. This journey redefined my life and myself. – Jenny Carmuciano

The saviour for me at the time was being surrounded by very positive people. They included my family: my parents, my brother and very close friends, who I regard as my family. Clients also provided much support. The world is very small these days, and people found out quickly that I was going through a divorce or the 'D' as I started to call it. There is such a stigma to being divorced still despite the fact that over 50 per cent of our population now fits the bill. A number of people I did not know well had found out and rang me. It was hard enough trying to separate out my feelings about my personal life from the daily workings of running a business, without feeling that even through my business my personal life was public property. It was uncomfortable to talk about but I had a statement ready: 'The relationship didn't work. I am trying to run a business and would really appreciate your patience'.

Really think about the team of people you surround yourself with. Who are they, what is the nature of your connection with them? Are they honest, positive, inspiring? Do they challenge you? The people you surround yourself with are so important to your business. – Katrina Webb

At the end of your life, you will know that nothing you have done matters – only who you have been while you have done it. – Neale Donald Walsch, Conversations with God

Lesson 3: find your release

I knew that if I did not take time out, and tried to cover up my feelings and not reflect on the journey, I might keep recreating the same experiences over and over again. This was a pattern which had repeated itself in my past relationships. I needed some time out. So for the next six months despite needing the money, I forced myself to work four days on average a week. I took time out. I joined a gym, which helped me release emotions that I otherwise may not have been able to. I went away by myself for a weekend for the first time in my life, and I howled and cried till I was sick. I wanted to grieve which I was struggling to do from my parents' spare room. I was trying to be strong for them by not showing many emotions, but emotions were building up the whole time.

I knew the whole time that if I didn't take time out, I would either burn out physically or worse still, lose hope.

Have you been through a major relationship break up? Or had a serious illness in your family? It doesn't matter how motivated and how excited you are about what you do in your work. When you're going through really tough times in your personal life, it affects what you do in your work, and how you do your work.

So don't pretend you're okay. Nurture yourself for once. Listen to your feelings. Take time out when it's needed and rest.

At this time in my life, I was struggling to sleep. I would wake up in the middle of the night after having gone to bed an hour before. By the time the alarm rang, I was exhausted and the day had not even started. This happened for days. Days turned into weeks. I would try and go to sleep and my head would be spinning. And this voice inside my head would be questioning my guilt, questioning what I was doing, and questioning my identity. This was hard, suddenly seeing the question 'who am I?' reappear in my life. I felt I'd lost part of my identity: the identity of a wife, of being part of a relationship, of being successful in all aspects of my life.

I had formulated that identity without thinking about the underlying meanings I had attached to it. As a woman, I don't think this is unusual – it's probably the way most of us think unless we stop to challenge those thoughts. But they're just not helpful. For example, I identified being single with not being as successful. I had the least money I'd had in a long time, and my underlying assumption for that was also 'I'm not successful'. I had to let go of these underlying assumptions that served me no purpose.

It was so much easier to change to a married name than to change it back. As I filled out tens and hundreds of forms to change my name, I made the decision to get business cards reprinted without my last name. I was questioning whether I should use my father's name or my ex-husband's. I decided I wanted to use *my* name – Shivani – because that part, at least, had not changed. So my business card till this day only has my first name on it. Very few people notice it and if they ask the question, I reply less seriously that it is my rock-star fantasy, and then explain my reason for being just me. No attachments.

I also had to focus on my sleeping problems and my feelings of being lost. When the bad sleeping pattern entered the second month, my brother, who's a doctor, said; 'I'm really worried about you and I'd like you to try some sleeping tablets'. I don't like sleeping tablets but on his insistence, I agreed to try them. I took them for four nights and I beat them every night – I still could not sleep. I then went onto conducted experiments – exercising up to four hours a day; drinking more than I usually did – but nothing was working. My mind was still racing.

Read personal development and self help books. Read them in the morning and read them before you sleep, make it a discipline. – Scott Anthony

When I was fourteen and had made my first trip to India after living in Australia for three years, my cousin who meditated every day had tried to teach me. I enjoyed it but once I came back to Australia, I did not want to be doing anything Indian any more, especially practices like meditation which were not widely accepted in Australia at the time. I thought people would see me as a 'weirdo' and the negative focus would return to me at school.

The significant problems we face cannot be solved at the same level of thinking we were at when we created them. – Albert Einstein

During this period of unrest, I met an amazing man who had been meditating for a couple of years. He suggested I approach his meditation teacher who could teach me to meditate. I was happy to try anything that might work at this stage. I committed to six sessions with the teacher, learning breathing and visualisation techniques. What came out of this process was absolutely brilliant. I learnt that meditation need not be a religious experience and that it was simply about quietening your mind. That was just what I needed. Finally, I started to sleep. Not the seven or eight hours I was used to, but more than four hours a night. It doesn't sound like much but it was a huge success after averaging only one or two hours a night for months.

The analogy that works for me is to imagine your mind like a bowl full of water. When the bowl is full, you cannot put any more water in it. You need to empty that bowl to allow it to be filled with new water. Our mind needs to be emptied in the same way if we want new thoughts, ideas and new ways of doing things to enter them.

Our work is full of yang: there is too much activity, too much busyness. We have to slow down. Meditation is yin, and it nourishes the soul.

Relaxation meditation is very easy

Sit for five to ten minutes a day in a quiet space.

> *Breathe in and out.*
>
> *Use any mantra: for example, 'I am breathing in positive energy' on inhalation and 'I am breathing out negative energy' on exhalation.*
>
> *Use the name of parents or kids or anything you like with each breath in and out.*
>
> *The point is to 'just stop!' If your mantra is taking up your concentration, there's no room left in your mind for the unceasing chatter.*

Since that period, meditation has become a part of my daily practice that allows me to clear my mind. As a result of that practice, my mind is not spending as much time on small activities and has become much more creative.

My cousin used to say when you are focusing on any activity, you can classify it as a form of meditation. You can apply this to almost anything, for example, the otherwise mundane task of washing dishes. You can begin to enjoy it by being mindful of what you are doing. You feel the warm water. The detergent that washes away the dirt. You think about how lucky you are for having dishes that you and your family can eat on. This is a form of meditation. If it sounds strange, try it!

> *When life gets 'full on' and you are running from one place to another, we need our releasers even more.*
>
> *My releasers are exercise and meditation. What are yours?*

Unless I am regularly exercising and meditating (which I do a minimum of five times a week each), my stress levels begin to rise and my tolerance levels start to dip. I have to balance that out because when I am stressed, I am no good to anybody.

One day when I was flying, the flight attendant was running through the safety check which I'd heard many times before but not ever really listened to. For the first time I got the symbolism. 'In case of an emergency, put your own mask on before you assist others.' To help others, you must help yourself first.

Put your own mask on first before assisting others because if you're no good, you are no good to anyone – Shivani

Lesson 4: keep it relative

Through regular meditation, my 'mental bowl' was being emptied regularly and it got thirsty for other materials – books in particular. I started to venture further into the area of self-development. As I scoured through self-development sections in bookshops, I found that I really enjoyed reading about other people's journeys, and in particular, those of people who had survived really tough times and made it.

Everything is relative. We have to feel the pain of our experiences to really move on, but then at some stage we have to dust ourselves off, reflect and take on board what we have learnt, and grow through the process.

One of the things that came of this was the decision to attend my first national speaking convention. There I met an extraordinary man who wrote a book called *It's Not What Happens To You, It's What You Do About It*. My life felt tough just then, as I was sitting next to him at dinner that night.

He had suffered burns to most of his body through a motorbike accident and survived against the odds. He had also been in a plane crash and survived! Why two major events like this happened to one person, I do not know but his attitude to life amazed me. He had no legs, no fingers and yet travelled around the world in a wheelchair, an international speaker in high demand. He could wow audiences of kids and adults equally. I found him incredibly inspiring and was touched when he gave me a copy of his book as a present.

This is not to underplay what I was going through, it's just to do a relativity measure. When I'm feeling down, I also think back to the children I met in Nepal and it makes my worries pale into insignificance.

Everything is relative. We have to feel the pain of our experiences to really move on, but then at some stage we have to dust ourselves off, reflect and take on board what we have learnt, and grow through the process.

Around the same time, I was working for the federal government, running workshops around Australia helping young kids learn about finances. I enjoyed this as it linked into a couple of my passions, working with kids in charities and working on boards.

I was running one such workshop, and having a very low day. I was just finalising the 'D' which was taking its toll on me physically and emotionally. A young man of seventeen, William, rocked up late to this workshop.

He swore a lot. In his examples, he would 'f' this and 'f' that. I could see the impact he was having on the rest of the group, who were starting to test the boundaries as well. This is no different than when I hang out with people who swear a lot – it rubs off on me.

I had to pull William aside. 'William, I'm really disappointed that you were late and that you are swearing away. The kids here are between fourteen and eighteen years old and if I start to lose control in this room, it's going to affect everybody and the rest of the workshop. You need to make a decision whether to stay and be polite or whether to go. What would you like to do?' William apologised, and replied 'I'll stay.'

After our 'pep talk' William shared with the group how he had got into drugs in his early teens and as a result had become a drug addict. He did not have any parents and had grown up in various foster homes. As a result of his drug habit, William got into some pretty heavy financial debt and he had decided to come to this workshop so he could learn how to manage his finances better. He was determined that he would get out of debt soon. The other kids really warmed to him, as I did.

In 1995 I found out I had a mild case of cerebral palsy on my right side. That then opened up all these new avenues where I could go to the Para-Olympic Games. From there I went and competed in Atlanta, Sydney and the Athens Para-Olympic Games and also a few World Championships and a Commonwealth Games over the last eleven or twelve years. I've won gold in 100 m, 200 m and 400 m sprints, as well as two silver and a bronze. – Katrina Webb

When lunchtime arrived, I was still in my 'victim' mode, just feeling blue about things in my personal life. I thanked William for sharing his experiences with some of the kids in the room. I said, 'Next door lunch is provided – there's hot food, sandwiches and orange juice. Why don't you go and have some?'

What William said next broke my heart. 'No thanks, Shivani. I only have enough to have one meal a day because I can't afford to have anything more. I don't want to teach my body that it can have more meals when it really is a one-off, so I'll give lunch a miss because the only meal that I have is dinner.' He smiled and went outside to enjoy the little sunshine that day away from the other kids.

After that conversation I went into the toilet and cried. William's attitude was amazing. He was an example of Maslow's hierarchy of needs, William's most basic needs were not being met. He had plenty of reasons to be in victim mode but for him they were non-existent.

Lesson 5: emotional intelligence

It is not what happens that matters, but rather it's how we interpret what happens that determines our emotions. The lesson I learned from William is the same one I stumbled across in Nepal – no matter what bad things happen to you in any given situation, it's up to you to choose how to view and react to that situation. The good news is that with increasing awareness of this, we can increase our ability to 'control' or choose our emotions.

> Our attitude is such an important part of how we live our lives, both in the professional and personal areas because we take our attitude with us wherever we go. – Shivani

We tend to experience the world and interpret it according to the mood we're in. In an experiment, a movie was shown of a face changing from happy to sad, with two groups of volunteers – one who'd described their state of mind as happy, and one that had described themselves as unhappy or depressed. Watching the face change, the happy volunteers saw the face remaining 'happy' looking for much longer than the unhappy lot.

When I am feeling down, the little negative voice inside me tells me I am no good. I try and fight this with some positivity but the little negative voice sometimes wins out.

My belief is that when you experience something positive, you will have a positive attitude towards that experience, person or situation. If you have a negative experience, you then form a negative attitude about that experience, person or thing.

For example, I attended a soccer game with one of my step-kids and the coach and some parents from the opposition side were yelling and swearing at their kids on the field. These kids are under twelve and I found this upsetting – so my perception about that opposition team was negative. Next time the kids played them, my attitude was 'I am not looking forward to this game'. And I recreated this experience. In this case, I have to work on my attitude so that I don't recreate the same experience.

What this means is that your feelings are a result of your conclusions about or interpretation of something that happens. Psychologist and writer, Cordelia Fine, discusses this concept in her research. If a customer gives you negative feedback then your interpretation or perception of that feedback will determine how you feel and consequently how you react. If your interpretation of the unhappy customer is: *she is unhappy because I am not good at my job* or *that happened to me at school as well and now no one will like me in this job either*, then you will feel pretty bad. If you see it as an opportunity to learn and improve and thank the customer for her feedback, it could be an event which actually leaves you inspired!

Think about your thoughts when you next feel good, bad, sad or happy. Understand the emotional thought that you've linked to the situation. If you're using negative thoughts, try and assess them honestly. Do you have to feel that way, or are you just choosing to?

> *Journaling is a great tool to help put things in perspective. It helps to release emotions on paper. It can also help us realise our negative thoughts or habits.*
>
> *Are your thoughts positive or negative? Acknowledge the negative ones and then work on consciously replacing the negative ones.*
>
> *If you're feeling particularly muddled or if things are not going well, try journaling every morning just after you get up. Write a couple of pages of whatever comes into your mind. Don't try to analyse it or even to make it all make sense – just write. You'll find that this method of 'dumping' thoughts really helps to clear your mind and focus you.*

In his book, *Emotional Intelligence*, Daniel Goleman developed the concept of Emotional Intelligence or EQ which includes 'self-awareness and impulse control, persistence, zeal and motivation, empathy and social deftness. These are qualities that mark people who excel: whose relationships flourish, who are stars in the workplace.'

Simply, it's about managing your emotions in a healthy way – not being overwhelmed by them, and equally not ignoring or squashing them. The elements that Goleman suggests make up Emotional Intelligence are self-management, motivation, social awareness and social skills.

When I looked at my own work practices in the light of the elements making up Emotional Intelligence, it became evident to me that I needed to work on keeping negative emotions under control. If I was working with a client who had negative staff, I tried not to judge them (which would mean getting caught up in their negativity). And, generally, if someone had a different point of view to me, I tried to have an understanding of their needs.

I also became more adaptable. If I had planned an agenda for the day and it needed to change to meet the clients' needs, then I did that. I worked at making myself part of the team I was working with at the time, rather than viewing myself solely as a consultant and them solely as the clients.

Sometimes the client had average standards but I ensured that I maintained my own standards while still giving them 100 per cent.

Being able to stand back and look at things in a new way was really helpful. Applying EQ became part of my way of operating and helped me to achieve my goals.

Lesson 6: working in partnership

There were many people I had come across that were very intelligent from an IQ perspective but they did not display some of the qualities of EQ. And as the business started to grow, I realised that I needed to partner up with some like-minded people who displayed both high IQ and EQ. I had the idea that I wanted to form some kind of business relationship with people who complemented my skills, and for whom I had complementary skills, so that they could not only help me, but I could also help them.

After doing some research, I started to approach various people who seemed like they might be a good fit. I'd meet up with them for a coffee, with the aim of determining their values and testing their like-mindedness. After meeting up with various people who didn't fit the bill, I met two men who had worked with large organisations and had been consulting for over ten years. We made a list of what each person wanted and found the common themes; we prepared a one-page document with the type of projects that we would work together on and what we would not. The informal agreement also covered profit share based on the amount each person did on each project rather than 50/50. It was the start of an associate model. Having a system that complements how you work together is essential.

I missed that group environment as well, I really work well in a group as part of a team. So I linked up with some commercial photographers in town to gain an office. It gave me that group environment and more social contact. – Jennie Groom

The associate model allowed for me to market to my clients that my business was now more than myself. It gave it credibility especially with some of the larger companies where the risk management was reduced – for example, if I was sick while working on a project, I could bring other people in. Best of all, I got a chance to bounce ideas around with others. I could finally also share the workload. Jointly, we responded to three government tenders, one of which we won based on our combined skill-set.

I had a mental model that said that unless I did it myself, it was no good. I was the best at what I did. Of course, rationally, I knew this wasn't true, but it was the way that I worked – unless I stopped, thought, and pulled myself up. However I realised at the point that the tender was delivered that I didn't need to be doing everything myself. I could tap into other people's experiences and expertise.

I hired a person, who was building an administration business of her own, to help me on a contract basis managing the bills, postage and other admin duties, which was really helpful.

Although the work she performed was excellent, the lesson that went with hiring the admin person was that her focus was the growth of her busienss and as the hours I needed fluctuated week to week, the clients that gave her more consistent work got in first!

People will partner with you to help you grow your business only if they are growing theirs, so look for opportunities that fulfil everyone's needs.

When partnering with people, their focus will be their business and how they grow their passion. If that is your focus too, then it is a win–win situation. But if there is another project that will help them deliver their vision more than working with you will, it makes business sense. People will partner with you to help you grow your business only if they are growing theirs, so look for opportunities that fulfil everyone's needs.

Let me share an example of a partnering relationship that I entered that didn't work and that I learnt much from. A company in the US approached me about helping them expand into Australia. We set up a teleconference and the company shared with me their vision of increasing their sales/revenue and market share.

At the time, I was operating from a place of fear. I was worried about money so I agreed to do it. I thought that I would do just enough, working on commission, to make around $10,000 per year through a little bit of sales and marketing. In hindsight knowing I was not that excited should have been my 'flag raiser' for the fact that this work did not fit my vision.

When I added up the hours I was spending organising their conference and various presentations to organisations on their behalf, I probably spent close to two months that year doing this work. One-sixth of my year doing what I did not love! I was not passionate about their products and their value-set was different to mine.

This period of two months of doing something I didn't love provided me with a very good list of pointers for next time, though:

Don't jump in head-first even when projects appear very good.

Look at the culture of the place that you are going to work in.
Do some investigation and research on the people and how they

operate. Then get smart and work out whether this opportunity is really for you.

Do a SWOT analysis in your business: look at your Strengths, Weaknesses, Opportunities and Threats. Prioritise the opportunities. Many opportunities will come knocking at your door and you have to know what you'll say 'no' to and what you'll say 'yes' to, based on your SWOT.

I still like to work too hard and need help with that. – Jennie Groom

Marketing and sales was a real challenge at the beginning. It was a role the old managing director had taken on so it was new work for us. The whole process of finding new customers was really quite scary. – Katrina Finlayson

Be self-aware, know your vision and your values before going into business. From this you need to address your weaknesses, really turn your liabilities into assets. – Katrina Webb

Lesson 7: networking 101

Since childhood, I'd had an entrepreneurial spirit. I loved talking to people and watching them as well. When I'd worked in the engineering world I'd made an observation that I'd never forgotten. When I compared an engineer who had exceptional technical skills but was not good at promoting themselves and their team with an engineer who had only sound technical skills but exceptional marketing skills, it would be the engineer with marketing skills who got most of the career advancements. I now believe this applies to all professions. It is very often not the best 'technical' person who gets the job, rather the one who is great at selling themselves.

My father is an example of this. He is an exceptional engineer – one of the smartest I've ever met – but could not sell his amazing attributes to his managers and peers. The biggest lesson he's had to learn in switching careers into financial planning is how to sell himself and now he is bringing in work through word of mouth, and helping people create wealth.

If you're outperforming the people around you, why wouldn't your career advance? As I started to attend more networking functions (and during the first couple of years, I went to the opening of almost anything), I learnt many things about networking.

Networking is such an important skill in business. Thinking back to the people who weren't as good as others but were winning a lot of work, I felt more strongly than ever that a successful business was a lot about the art of selling yourself!

If you've got the technical skills – whether that technical skill set is constructing websites, hairdressing, cooking, engineering, writing or whatever – it's how you market and network your skills that gets you known and brings you more work … unless you are the world expert in that area!

But before you rush into your next networking encounter, there's one more very important thing. Networking needs to be done in an authentic way to be effective. I encountered a hilarious example while I was running a networking session for an association of chartered accountants. The session was for middle-level managers, and there were about 100 people in the room.

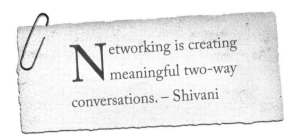

Networking is creating meaningful two-way conversations. – Shivani

After my keynote presentation, I gave the accountants a form and suggested it was time to practise the philosophies I had shared. Their task was to find five people in the room they'd never met and then ask them a series of questions including their name, whether they had children, their favourite sport to watch and play, if they had a pet, the pet's name, and so forth.

What I saw in the next five minutes was astounding. Each person would walk awkwardly to another and ask in a monotone, ticking off the sheet as they went along, 'What's your name? What's your business? Do you have a pet? What's the pet's name?' Once they had their checklist answered, they would move on unemotionally towards their next victim!

This was a disaster. I had to grab the microphone and stop the whole exercise, and tell them: 'This is not the point. When you are networking with a task in mind, the first priority is to engage with the person you are talking to. You have to care about that person otherwise any information you get from them is just data – and they'll be aware of that. You have to convert your wish for data into an approach that is focused on getting to know this person. You want to ask those questions with genuine interest in the other person but you don't want to have the form in front of you, that is just something you fill out after you have the conversation, so just have a *meaningful* conversation.'

This got many of them out of their comfort zones but as they completed the task, I could see them starting to enjoy themselves, as it felt more real and more natural.

Data ›› Information ›› Knowledge ›› Wisdom

While I was confident that I could run the business, I was less confident to sell and network and get out there by myself talking to people about the business and approaching people. It was quite a jump for me. – Abbie Martin, Lifestyle Elements

At this point, although I could help out the accountants, I realised that I needed to learn more about networking to really move to a different level myself. One of the things I did was to research how people network. It appeared to me that different cultures networked differently. The one that fascinated me the most was the comparison between the US and Australia. In Australia, we are more laid back and find it hard to talk about ourselves. In the US, people are much better trained to talk about themselves and it's much more *acceptable* to talk about yourself.

I also found interesting differences in networking in a smaller city and larger cities. Even within the same culture, people have differing values.

For example when McDonald's entered the Indian market they did not sell beef burgers. Why? Because Hindus (the predominant religion in India) believe that the cow is a sacred animal. This shows McDonald's understanding of India's culture – by knowing how to position and network themselves in that country, they not only avoid offending people and poor sales, but instead turn it around and make great sales of other products.

So, when you're networking it's almost the same. You've got to understand the culture that you're networking in. If you are doing a presentation in the country, the people are generally pretty relaxed. You may not need to do a formal presentation in your best corporate suit. You must act and dress accordingly to the culture you are operating in.

I tend to change my language slightly to suit the culture. If I'm talking to students, I don't wear a suit. I want them to know that I'm approachable, that I am like them. I will wear a denim jacket to fit into their culture. Now that doesn't mean I have to go and act like a fifteen year old – but I want to talk *at their level*. I want to make sense to them. Equally, when I am networking in a corporate environment, I'll dress in a suit and my language will be more formal to suit the environment. This is the art of communication and networking.

When people think of networking, they often think of the business world. But it's a mistake to believe that if you're not operating in that environment that networking doesn't apply to you. Of course it does. Take the example of a fish and chip shop – how does a business like this network?

A fish and chip shop has many stakeholders with whom they network. There's the shop owner next door, suppliers, and there are also issues like parking places, which might mean networking with the local council or other business owners. If the shop owner next to you has complementary products, you may be able to work out a deal with them offering a package to customers, for example, drinks next door! So you're networking all the time!

Think back to the concept of emotional intelligence. Simply, humans network as a matter of course – it's what we do. In a business sense, as in any other sense, how well we network depends on how well we manage our social skills and our relationships with others. Don't be like the accountants (although let me add that they are wonderful people who have simply not been trained in networking) in the example above, just trawling for benefits to you or for data that you need. A good relationship goes a long way.

When I go to cafés, I choose the place that has good coffee and fantastic service where they remember my name and my order over a place that has exceptional coffee and poor service. This provides a good clue to café owners in terms of how important customer service and keeping customers are. The good ones – the ones that 'network' well – are the ones that care about their customers and know simple things like their customers' names and what coffee they drink. Is it any wonder that most cafés go bust within five years?

Trust was really important between us and the client so developing a relationship where we could discuss easy and tough subjects was what we came to focus on. – Katrina Finlayson

It doesn't matter whether you are a small business that's in the start-up phase or whether you've been going for a few years. You've got to go back to first principles and ask:

Who are my stakeholders?

Who am I networking with?

How am I building relationships?

Do I understand the culture of the people that I'm building relationships with?

Chapter 4

Year 3: consolidation and problem-solving

Interesting people ❦ Abundance mentality ❦ Karma ❦
Think bigger – think outside the square ❦ Your unique place
in the marketplace ❦ Dealing with the media ❦ Alliances
and associates ❦ Diversity and Synergy ❦ Ethics, principles
and values ❦ Negative beliefs ❦ The competitive world

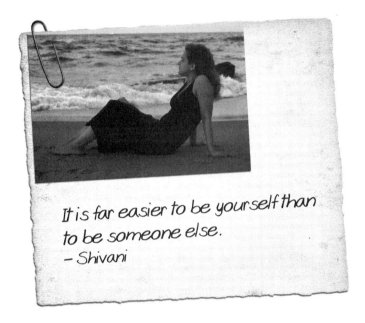

It is far easier to be yourself than to be someone else.
– Shivani

uring my third year, I was starting to see and feel some real changes manifesting, not just in my daily routine, but also in the type of people I was attracting. Jack was one who made my life richer by his presence.

Lesson 1: karma and the abundance mentality

Jack was 71 and still working. I asked him why. He had been CEO of a large company, which he'd built up and then sold off for quite a handsome sum. He was still working three days a week, not for the money, but he enjoyed using his brain, he told me. He acted as a consultant to his old business and also to other clients, three days a week.

It was really important to Jack that he and his wife had some separation around hobbies and activities; this meant they had something to talk about at the end of the day. I was impressed and thought what a great example of never 'retiring' from life. We all need to feel needed, useful, that we're contributing and that our relationships are thriving.

Another interesting fact about Jack was that he was giving much of his time back to the community. He had an abundance mentality. He believed that because he had been so blessed, he wanted to give something back. He also believed that good things happen to good people. His general outlook was very positive. His positive energy rubbed off on me and I found it a pleasure working with him.

A recent book by Stephen Post and Jill Neimark, *Why Good Things Happen to Good People* suggests that giving is one of the most potent ways for us to experience wellbeing. The book's subtitle says it all: 'The exciting new research that proves the link between doing good and living a longer, healthier, happier life'. Post and Neimark quote many studies backing up the power of giving and doing good, and in Jack, I can see a living example of this philosophy.

> *My greatest achievement through this change in direction is what I have been able to learn about myself, a big part of which has been the lesson 'do unto others as you wish them to do unto you'. Seeing students succeed in what they are doing and receiving gratitude for the part I play in teaching that is a fantastic achievement for me.*
> *– Nikki Seymour-Smith*

Giving reduces depression, and it's far more powerful than receiving. Giving to others helps us to forgive ourselves for our own 'mistakes'.

This is something called a 'helper's high'. Post and Neimark quote a study in which 50 per cent of helpers reported feeling a high when they helped others, while 43 per cent felt stronger and more energetic.

For me the real achievements are what I see in my clients. Watching people achieve their goals and regain their health is wonderful. Examples are helping people rise out of depression, or helping people with Multiple Sclerosis regain motor skills and do things such as drive a car again. I specialise in pre-conception work with women and couples and it seems every time I have clients fall pregnant through the therapies I really feel a great deal of emotion. These small victories that I am able to experience regularly are what I feel are my greatest successes and achievements. – Kylie Armstrong

Some years ago there was a study done in the UK aimed at finding out what professions provided most satisfaction. Interestingly, small business owners came out on top. When asked about the main reason for their sense of satisfaction, they mentioned things like the sense of completing useful tasks, 'helping' their customers, and hearing and seeing their appreciation. I found that the opinions of those interviewed for this book – all from various backgrounds and running their own businesses – corresponded with those from the UK study. When asked what their greatest successes and achievement have been, the majority responded that appreciation from the customer gives them the deepest ongoing sense of satisfaction!

When I have someone approach me after a talk or I receive an email from someone I've worked with, it gives me the greatest sense of pleasure. I put it into my 'feel good' folder.

Try it yourself.

Create a 'feel good' folder for any appreciative cards, emails or notes you receive.

Give daily in small ways. It doesn't have to be material – think about all the different ways you can give, or do good. Pay someone a compliment on an outfit; praise a junior member of staff; do a favour for a friend.

When I have someone approach me after a talk or I receive an email from someone I've worked with, it gives me the greatest sense of pleasure. I put it into my 'feel good' folder.

We have always known the value of doing good. I grew up in a household and in a culture and religion that talked a lot about karma, but it was never something I fully understood. When I googled it I found a definition that said: 'for every event that occurs there will follow another event whose existence was caused by the first and this second event will either be pleasant or unpleasant according to the cause that was good or not good'. That's a bit roundabout, but I understand it to be saying that when we do good, even though we might not get the karmic effect of that in a positive way straight away, it will happen. And, turning the coin on the other side, if we do something that is not good, then that will catch up with us also, although maybe not straight away.

I found a great discussion about karma in *The Law of Karma* by Phra Bhasakorn Bhavilai. I began to see that it's not wise to force things to happen; some things will happen in time. And we have to be humble enough not to challenge the timing!

Karma has helped me in business by allowing me to see the benefits of helping people who I may not get any direct help back from. I might advise a student on his or her career options, or help someone who is looking to start a business by providing them with assistance and mentoring, or give another coach working in the same industry the title of a book that has really helped my coaching. Doing this makes me feel great. I know that with each bit of good I have done, the karma has come back two or three times better from other people.

Lesson 2: marketing yourself

> If you're good, people tell others and if you're not good, people tell others. So be good! – Shivani

This year also saw me starting to think bigger. My business had started to grow in the areas of consulting, coaching and speaking. Law firms brought me a lot of work this year. I came to the realisation that the 'power of the word' spreads quickly. It felt like karma – I'd been working so hard, and it did seem as if somehow some of the fruits of all that work were coming to bear, as I began to get more referrals and new clients.

As a result of other clients doing my marketing for me by recommending me, a large law firm asked me to organise a leadership conference for their senior associates. This really stretched my mind as I had not operated on this scale before and had to think more creatively.

> *Don't assume you need to go and pay for advertising or marketing. There is so much free marketing out there. Do a short course in marketing and get an initial idea and a broad understanding. Marketing equals 'building relationships'. – Abbie Martin*

Got a challenge? Meet it head on …

> *Ensure that you have people around you who can help you generate 'outside the square' thinking.*
>
> *Let the ideas fly before you sort them into some kind of order. Don't interrupt the creative process.*
>
> *Bring in others to help you. It's not admitting defeat – it's ensuring that you'll provide a quality service.*

As I did not have enough material to keep twenty senior associates from all over Australia busy for three days and did not generally work weekends, I decided to bring in other experts in a creative way to help facilitate this leadership retreat/workshop. This also followed the principle of helping others and creating relationships and good karma.

> *Surround yourself with those that know more than you. This will help you grow and learn, and be prepared to accept information and teachings. – Nick Palousis*

Work–life balance was a major issue for this firm. These 'Gen X' lawyers were very career-minded, but also believed in having a good work–life balance. They saw their senior partners work very long hours, which compromised Generation X's values, but left them unsure how to get ahead in the corporate world without following the same path.

So when thinking about bringing other people in, I thought about facilitators with skill-sets not only complementary to mine, but people who would tap into the work–life balance issue. I included instructors for morning yoga classes before the day began and a specialist team-building facilitator who conducted outdoor activities reflecting the culture of the organisation. We also had debriefs following the various activities. I also arranged for a keynote speaker to give an after-dinner talk.

When we take small steps, we gain confidence and motivation in achieving bigger goals. – Shivani

Part of my aim in successfully putting this leadership conference together was to attain a deep understand of the leadership needs and initiatives this firm was wanting to put into practice. The experience gave me the motivation to know I could organise things at a larger scale.

My tips for staying creative and daring:

Think big and act with courage and calculate your risk.

Think laterally when it comes to product or service.

Don't let, 'it has never been done before' stop you.

Don't share a great idea with everyone. Nurture it first, let it grow and then protect it as intellectual property.

Read the business gurus and find out what they did.

Get away from your business to assess things from a distance.

Use brainstorming for idea-generation with staff, other businesses and trusted customers.

Develop customer survey forms – and act on the information!

Think long term and keep building relationships.

Ensure that you value creative thinking in your business, and reward your employees for it.

Be resilient.

Out of this initial foray into running a big workshop came my dream to run a sold-out conference for women. I wanted it to have exceptional speakers, to be aimed at all levels, from junior employees to directors, and to be reasonably priced. My experience in the corporate world was very few conferences were held for women and the ones that did exist were expensive and impossible for, say, a PA to attend. So it was important to market the conference to women as useful, relevant and reasonably-priced. And I was clear that the theme for the conference would be 'balance', an area that women find challenging to juggle. Putting into practice experience from the law firm workshop, I rang speakers who I thought would inspire women into action.

As the thinking got bigger, I realised it was also going to cost bigger money. My fears started to rise. I thought of sponsorship but didn't allow enough time for it to eventuate. Tickets were not selling as fast as I had hoped. Many people had told me they were interested but had not sent their registration forms. Spurred on by my fears about money, I got out and started to ring individuals and companies I had worked with. I cleared my diary to focus on this.

> *Fear does pop up. It is natural. We're all human.*
>
> *The trick is to learn to deal with it when it does arrive. Take action – and you'll feel better.*

In the end with the help of an event manager, we made it and sold out a few days before the conference. And the morning of the conference when I walked on stage to greet the 220 women who attended, I felt elated!

As a result of the conference, I had 'invested' over $10,000 from my own pocket after expenses were paid. But with the conference in full swing, many women approached me, and thoughts of money went out the window. Women even wrote to me afterwards sharing how life-changing the conference had been for them! Every cent and minute was worth it. I knew this would help me create good karma.

> *I never give up, that is how I have encouraged our studio to apply their work in broader ways such as film, mining and simulation. I was not initially successful in getting them to do it, so I flew to China to the studios and our head office to explain to them how to do it, and to sell the idea to them. I am also a lateral thinker, which is what is behind my new directions with the company. I would say too I am very driven but also creative. – Ruchi Goel*

Later, I was approached by a person running the state arm of a national training business to facilitate leadership workshops for them, which I agreed to do. However I ended up confusing the marketplace. Some of my clients were in the workshop, which meant that suddenly they were seeing me in a different guise. It didn't work particularly well for my business. When running your business, you have to get clear on your role and how you want to be seen in the market you operate within.

Lesson 3: media smarts

Working with various clients including an advertising agency, the media picked up on some of the work I was doing, and I was approached for an interview and article to be published on my business.

I was so pleased. This is the cheapest form of advertising a business can have! During the interview, I was asked about the type of work I was doing, and the names of some of the clients I was working with.

Having sought permission, I mentioned some of the organisations I was working with. In the article that followed in print, it read 'Shivani is currently working with clients who are in trouble…' And then, to add insult to injury, the name of the advertising agency was mentioned.

I was appalled at how the words had been minced to make the story sound more interesting. The chairman of the advertising agency felt the same way and called me.

The business had a right to be upset as the work we were doing was proactive and they were not in any kind of trouble. However, the article implied that they were, and the chairman was worried about customers' perceptions.

I wrote a formal letter of apology to the board, but I needed to manage the relationship with the media as well. I communicated to them that I was very grateful for the opportunity, but that my client was very upset with the comment that had been published, which was misleading, and that I would appreciate a written apology as I did not make that comment.

Eventually the journalist made an apology which was printed in the publication.

Most of the media I have worked with are excellent. If there is however a way to proof an article before it goes to press so that you can double–check it, then I would definitely recommend it.

> *Articles and profiles in the press are a great – and very cheap – way of marketing.*
>
> *Find out who the various business writers are in your local media. By building a relationship with them, you can perhaps write an occasional article for them, and they can ring you for comment, keeping your name in the news even when you're not being profiled.*

For example, I'd like to write articles on women in business in *The Australian* and the *Business Review Weekly*, so I am currently in the process of establishing relationships which will help me to achieve that.

Lesson 4: you can't do it all yourself

Creating alliances and associate relationships are important. I had begun developing these in my second year, but at this point I knew that these alliances needed a revisit from a strategic perspective. I was still finding it hard to pass work on and needed to ensure that I was delegating tasks to others rather than doing all the basic things myself.

> *Another success for me has been the Tribe, a network of professionals combined by a code of ethics and a commitment to working together as*

In the first two and a half years I did most things. I was the director, cleaner, facilitator, marketer, director and PA. And the list goes on. It was ridiculous!

a team to bring clients the best result, across the marketing spectrum. It was a cross referring sort of network, but it has become more powerful than that yet more streamlined than a huge agency. This is perhaps my most proud achievement. – Janelle Gerrard

For example, at one point I had been thinking about becoming accredited to conduct Myers-Briggs personality profiling. Then I realised that rather than go through the process of accreditation myself I should be utilising other people to conduct the tests. I started to ask myself, 'Do I need to do this myself? Is someone else going to add more value to this than me? Would I better serve myself by using the time to work on other things?' A lot of the time the answer was yes, so I started to outsource some work.

In the first two and a half years I did most things. I was the director, cleaner, facilitator, marketer, director and PA. And the list goes on. It was ridiculous!

Michael Gerber, author of *The E-Myth*, a useful book about making small businesses work, emphasises the importance of systems when you start running your own business. He suggests – even if you're a one-man or one-woman band – that you still do an organisational chart of what the business will look like once it's bigger. Initially it may be your name in all of the boxes. Nonetheless, this exercise will help you to understand and value all the different hats you wear.

> *Try it yourself.*
>
> *Set out an organisation chart putting down every single kind of role that the business utilises and how much time each one takes. It doesn't matter if there aren't staff to fill those roles.*
>
> *Also think about what roles or functions will be necessary for the business to expand.*

Now do a position description for each position you've created on your chart.

Doing both these things will not only give you an idea of the scope of the business but will also help give you a clear idea of who you need to hire when you're in a position of adding staff.

As my business started to grow, I became more creative. Some small tasks which were repetitive work like paying the bills and typing notes could be done systematically by others who enjoyed that type of work – leaving me free to do what I was best at!

Lesson 5: managing a healthy workplace culture

Bringing in others has other benefits as well as freeing yourself up. One of these is the ability to tap into *synergy*. This is a principle which states that the whole is greater than the sum of its parts.

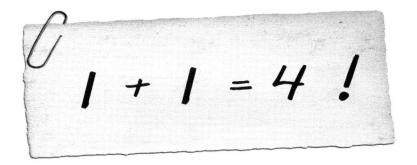

Naturally we do not just achieve synergy simply by having more bodies around; the components need to work harmoniously together. True synergy is reached through a combination of the information possessed by individual employees, their ability to act appropriately on that information, and their ability and willingness to share it with the rest of the organisation.

Carl Rogers, an influential American psychologist, said: 'That which is most personal is most general'. We know how we can gain trust and deepen the conversation by being open, admitting perhaps a weakness or a low point. The more authentic we become, the more others feel safe enough to also open up.

In a workplace context, this means admitting mistakes or weaknesses, feeling safe enough to look silly or ask silly questions. In a sense it's about allowing everyone to be themselves – because when you feel able to be your authentic self, you're more likely to achieve something special. This level of trust and openness is necessary for maximising creativity and for synergy.

> *Your people are your business, they share the ownership, the vision and the work, and understanding this is an authentic part of myself that I feel is really valuable. – Julian Burton*

Marcus Buckingham and Donald O Clifton, authors of *Now Discover Your Strengths* believe that a great organisation must not only accommodate the fact that each employee is different, it must capitalise on these differences.

> *Your capacity is related to your capability and your passion.*
>
> *You can learn to be competent in almost anything.*
>
> *Your weakness is the best opportunity to grow.*

I worked with one client that had an excellent leadership model, but they were experiencing a very large turnover and did not understand why. This made me curious. This was an organisation with a great culture. For example, when I would visit the CEO, he would make me coffee at the front desk rather than ask the receptionist to do it. This practice flowed through the organisation and each of them was trained to make brilliant coffees!

As I sat in various meetings, I was impressed by the engagement of the employees and would consider them to be in the top quartile of businesses I worked with. So what I couldn't understand was why, despite this very tight and wonderful culture, there was such a high turnover.

I talked to their HR manager and decided to conduct one-on-one interviews to find out more. I also arranged to interview four employees who had recently left the company.

Our most valuable resource is our people, so get good staff and look after them and let them know what the business needs to do to improve. – Simone Preston

By the third interview, it had become obvious that the culture was perhaps *too* tight. People felt stifled. Most of the long-standing staff had grown into the culture and hence the turnover had been low. As the business had expanded, the new people felt like they were in a closely protected family – and as they were not used to this culture, they found it difficult. They referred to it as a 'fraternity', saying that if you went against it or questioned its practices, you were made to feel disloyal. In the end, they decided to leave. Most of the people who had left in the last two years were newcomers.

It's really great to have a tight and aligned culture as long as there is room for people who are different and as long as their individual contributions are valued. If people don't want to hang out on a Friday night with their colleagues for a drink, they should not be considered disloyal.

We naturally tend to value what we ourselves are good at, so it is in our nature to reject other ways as wrong – but thinking this way in the workplace is not conducive to encouraging all employees to do their best. If people don't feel that they're performing at their peak, it's likely that the company won't be performing at its peak, either – as the organisation is nothing more than a sum of its employees.

Lesson 6: don't forget your values

I was working with a casino looking at their leadership competencies and helping them formulate their culture at a senior level. The project had many complexities and was going to take three months to complete. My first point of call was to walk around and get a 'feel' for the place and its culture, so I arranged a meeting to do a 'meet and greet' and to walk around the organisation.

As I walked through the casino where their customers were playing poker machines and engaging in other forms of gambling, something churned inside me. Something was not resonating with me. Something did not feel right.

I realised that feeling was telling me that the products this business offered did not feel right to me.

> *Are they a legitimate business? Absolutely!*
>
> *Is gambling a choice? Absolutely!*
>
> *Do a lot of casinos put money back into the community to help in preventing gambling addictions? Absolutely!*

Valuing my clients and them valuing me is important and doing so has continued to assist the business and develop it. – Simone Preston

I want to be clear that the company and the people within it are excellent – but my value-set did not match with the product.

If your business was to go and sing songs, you'd pick songs that you liked, right? You wouldn't sing songs that don't resonate with you at all. Likewise, it is important to have true passion but also to have a clear idea of your ethics in a business.

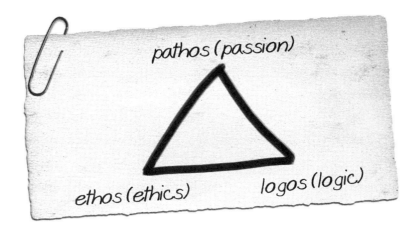

As a result, I made a list of companies I don't want to work with – tobacco, casinos, environmentally harmful companies and arms dealers. When you start to define what you will and won't do, you get clearer about who you really are, what you will stand up and fight for, and what you are prepared to let go.

One of the most important things is the type of client you attract and target – you want someone who values you. – Kylie Armstrong

Also at around this time a government client had asked me to set up a leadership program for their managers. I was looking forward to this work. Towards the end of the presentation as I was listing the total of what I could provide, they cut me off.

Two of the three directors told me that their limited budgets could not afford me but that they really wanted me. They also claimed that there was potentially more work in the pipeline … and suggested that doing this project for half of what I normally charge would be a good strategic move. I felt the McDonald's experience recurring. However, as I wanted to do more work with government departments, I reluctantly agreed to a lower rate.

Hindsight is a wonderful thing. In hindsight I should have said no – so why did I say yes? Because I did not feel worthy of charging that amount as I could see they believed they had lower budgets than my clients in private enterprise. Nobody had questioned my prices before, which I took to mean that they were reasonable. Suddenly being questioned about them and not having an answer prepared, I cracked and accepted a lower fee without proper consideration of its effect on my business.

The lesson here is in knowing your worth. If a client can't afford you, then it is okay to say 'no'. If it is a not-for-profit organisation that you want to contribute to, then that is a different decision and you may decide to do it for nothing.

> *If a client says they cannot afford you, or is being stingy with their money, don't assume you are not worth what you normally charge.*

This learning also applied to my keynote speaking. When I first started speaking through the awards process, I was excited at just being asked. As I started to get more requests to speak at schools and corporations, my time started to get consumed. I could not afford to talk for four or five days a week when I was not bringing an income in for that time. Some of the award-winners worked for employers who gave them support in speaking engagements – as it was good marketing for the businesses, and the speaker was still earning a salary while speaking. However because I was running my own business, I was actually losing money when I was speaking.

At first, I took whatever was given to me, whether it was $100, $50 or $300.

As I've learnt more about speaking, I realise now that I was sending out conflicting messages, and being unfair to my clients by charging them different prices. Everybody talks – and you don't want the people who paid you $300 speaking to the people who paid you $50 and feeling ripped off.

I am not talking about picking a number out of the air. You must do your benchmarking, work out what your competitors are charging, and ask what your clients are paying for similar services. By asking questions as you come across people, you will get a sense of what to charge.

My rule for a new product or service is to ask around fifteen or twenty people. Sometimes in a conversation at a networking event, I will ask a speaker, 'which bureaus do you find work best for you? I am listed with Xyz Speakers' Bureau. What sort of pricing works in different markets for you?'

People who are established and come from a place of abundance will share this with you – as it provides them with a benchmark also. (Of course if you're asking for information, it's also fair to offer some back!) The pricing strategy for your business can start as simply as that.

Lesson 7: challenge your negative beliefs

I've seen many women struggle to ask for what they really believe they are worth. And I've heard too many stories about women who, like I did, have relented when challenged, and become resentful later.

So I built this into my sessions when working with clients, creating a conversation or role-play to broach the issue of dealing with money if a client brings it up.

Lynne Franks in her book *Grow: The Modern Woman's Handbook* discusses how women treat money:

> We women are seldom paid the same as men, even when we're quite high up on the job ladder, but it's up to us to ensure that we ask for what we want and deserve.

Franks also asserts that women making choices because they *want* to do other things is OK, but when it comes to money, women should charge what they are entitled to.

The CEO of a large government department asked me to look at why there was such a low representation of women at senior levels in that organisation. This was a very exciting project that included collation of information in three forms – electronically surveying, focus groups and one-on-one discussions with women in senior roles. The electronic surveying was done in collaboration with an IT company who designed five key questions that were sent out in an email, with the responses then being automatically collated. This was a time-saving exercise for the approximately 300 women I expected to respond.

However over a thousand women responded, and the overall findings were:

> A third of them did not want to move into senior-level positions. This highlighted an assumption that if someone did not want to move up to the next level, they weren't career-minded and therefore that investing in such a person was a waste of money. But many women in this category enjoyed the ability to work flexibly as they had young families, or were simply content with their work and output at this level. They felt judged that they did not want to move up the corporate ladder!

> Twenty percent of women had tried for senior positions, had not succeeded, and had given up trying again.

> The other 50 per cent or so did not feel good enough to even try to attain more senior positions.

This was very interesting because several of these responses come down to attitude and self-belief.

I found it particularly interesting that 50 per cent of the women surveyed did not know how to market themselves and felt that they were not good enough to get to the next level, because when coaching women I've found that this was a very common issue or belief.

Many, many women – me included – have a common set of attitudes or beliefs that conflict with their feelings of having a right to succeed:

- Fear of failure
- Fear of success
- Not wanting to demand more help at home from their partner in order to take on more senior or demanding roles
- Procrastination (for example, 'I will do something once the kids grow up')
- Lack of time
- Low self-esteem
- Negative outlook
- Being a perfectionist
- Scared of risk-taking
- Lack of money
- Not enough confidence
- Giving up too soon
- Laziness
- Not wanting to be seen as 'bossy' or as having male characteristics
- Introverted
- Too shy
- Always wanting to be liked
- Living out past mistakes
- Not wanting to give up on being 'everything' in the family

Performance is not affected by your level of education, your gender, age, health or intelligence. The most important determiner is that you believe that you can do it and then do what it takes!

The greatest discovery of my generation is that a human being can alter his life by altering his attitudes. – William James

Self-educate so you can foster your own growth. Books, DVDs, websites, whatever you can get your hands on. – Simone Preston

Which of the three categories do you fit into?

- happy as you are
- tried and failed
- don't think you'd make it so haven't tried

What is holding you back from trying?

As a result of the project, the organisation undertook the recommendation to run self-esteem workshops targeting in particular the 50 per cent of the women in the survey who had the belief that they weren't good enough to try for senior-level positions.

I'd like to share a story with you as an analogy to the above survey. Most people have been to a circus, and many of us have seen elephants performing in the circus. When an elephant is trained as a baby, one of the things that the circus owners do is put a metal chain around one of his legs and the chain is staked. The elephant can walk around in a big circle – depending on the length of the chain. When the elephant tries to step out of the circle, the metal around his leg has sharp spokes which bite into his flesh and he gets hurt and bleeds. The pain teaches him to stop pushing his boundaries beyond the length of the metal chain.

As elephants grow up, they learn not to take risks. I remember vividly seeing an adult elephant when I was a kid at a circus which had a flimsy rope tied around its leg. I didn't question it then but I now know that a grown-up elephant could very easily break the rope and run away – but it doesn't because the length of the rope is, in the elephant's mind, the same as a steel chain. So his attitude is that 'if I go beyond that point, then I will get hurt'.

This taught me to look at my own 'invisible rope'. I'd formed some beliefs and attitudes about various things and had stopped venturing outside my circle of comfort, just like the elephant. I also realised that some of my beliefs and values were not my own but my parents', although I had thought they were mine until I examined them closely.

Think about it this way. A baby's learning how to walk and falls over. Does the mother then say 'that's it, you've tried seventeen times and fallen over. I don't think you are worthy of walking ever again'? Of course she doesn't. So why do we say it to ourselves?

What is your attitude towards career advancement?

What are your attitudes and beliefs in other parts of your life?

Is there an 'invisible rope' that is holding you back?

This is something which is really important to look at. If you've tried before and that hasn't worked – does that mean you never try again?

I met a woman called Helen who was doing a PhD on women in golf. Helen explained that women feel guilt when agreeing to play golf because they don't consider it networking – they see it as 'time out of the office', or wasted time. Men on the other hand felt that it was okay, and that it's their right to play golf and use it as a networking opportunity.

Are there some activities you don't do out of fear?

I avoided playing golf till I met Helen. I was always an ordinary golfer (ordinary = awful in my mind). When I went to play in an Ambrose Event for a charity day, I picked up an enormous amount of work. So I have to say, networking at golf events really works. That does not mean that women have to do everything masculine but instead that as a woman you need not be scared of trying something like golf.

Lesson 8: don't fear the competition

A real estate firm approached me to coach five of their senior sales staff. I had been increasingly enjoying doing more work with women. Although one of my fears was being perceived in a negative way as 'just a feminist' by the large number of men who run organisations, I wanted to focus on coaching women.

I found marketing myself was really tough. – Simone Preston

When I met these five women they were all gorgeous and ranged in age. They dressed well, drove fancy cars, had great faces and bodies and spoke well. Part of it is simply a requirement for their industry – no one wants someone shabby in an old car to come and sell their house!

In spite of this, four out of five had the belief that they were not very good-looking, along with having a general lack of belief in their capabilities. This is despite them being senior salespeople who were making very good money for their organisation and for themselves. Additionally, most of them struggled with working in isolation.

Although the company had a large number of employees, the women felt that they were competing with each other. They loved their job but wanted the culture to be more collaborative.

We need to be able to connect. If we can't, our emotional processes can become defeatist.

I worked with these women using concepts similar to those discussed in Richard Hill's *How the 'Real World' Is Driving Us Crazy*. Hill outlines his beliefs about what living in a competitive environment does to us, and defines seven 'demons' of our competitive world-view. These demons, which he believes interfere with and disrupt our enjoyment of life through causing stress, are:

Right and wrong	*Good and bad*
Expectation	*Fault and blame*
Criticism	*Isolation and separation*
Guilt	

The black-and-white, winner–loser world that Richard Hill describes is based on the principle of 'every man for himself'.

Humans are social animals. We *need* to be able to connect. If we can't, our emotional processes can become defeatist. This was more than evident in the real estate agents I was working with. Although they longed for social contact, and *not* to be in competition with each other, when these things weren't happening, their thought processes were becoming negative and self-critical.

Hill describes various thoughts that stem from isolation and separation:

- I am different
- No one loves me
- Unless I am number one, there is no point
- No one really likes a winner/loser
- People are just all out for themselves
- No one can be trusted
- You are always hurt by the ones you love
- I get no respect from anyone
- As soon as you open up to someone they will use it and leave you.

I discussed with the women what they would like to create, what relationships they wanted to nurture, and who they wanted to collaborate with. Together we planned how to realise this. As a result of the coaching, they were able to achieve their aims and their sales improved!

Chapter 5

Year 4: finding balance and taking risks

The importance of education ❧ Choosing work strategically
❧ Personality profiling ❧ Learning to say 'no' without fear
❧ Learning to say 'yes' without fear ❧ Becoming a coach

Education
is freedom
– Shivani

Year four was absolutely fantastic both on a personal and business front. Starting to build up a lot more confidence in myself was now starting to pay dividends. I had also been involved in giving back to the community through sitting on two not-for-profit committees and boards which was bringing me much satisfaction. Most of my peers on this committee and board were rich and retired and I was pleased that I did not have to wait till then to be able to contribute.

Lesson 1: finding pleasure in work

Once people are educated, irrespective of which country or society they're living in, they have choice and freedom. This idea is important to me in several ways: one, because I'd done some work with university students in the past, and found it tremendously enriching, and two, because it ties in with my wish to be able to spend time working on things I enjoy, whether they be paid or unpaid.

I was keen on doing more work with students, helping to educate them in areas such as networking and marketing themselves, career opportunities, becoming an entrepreneur, and improving work–life balance.

As a result of the work, I was awarded an honorary membership to the Golden Key Society. Honorary Members are elected by local Golden Key chapters and are individuals who are active on campus or in the community. These honorary members – including dignitaries such as Bill Clinton and Ian Thorpe – reflect the qualities and values of Golden Key members and are active in areas of scholarship, leadership or services. So it was an honour to join such an extraordinary list!

Equally as important to me is having time for a personal life, and not being entirely consumed by work. It is sometimes difficult to separate your personal life from your professional life, and it is important to make sure that there is an overlap and that you continue to look after both sides.

During this year I met an extraordinary man; it was almost like I'd known him before. He was the soulmate I had desired for a long time.

He was someone who understood me and had a similar value-set to me, and he encouraged me to be true to my passion of working with more women. I was beginning to realise the impact of my coaching through the amazing positive feedback I had received. Many of the women had become friends after the formal coaching process had finished. Others ring me months and years later to let me know of their latest victory in their personal or business life, which still brings tears to my eyes.

From coaching I learnt that it is not about me being an expert. I felt enriched from each interaction in a coaching relationship. You give, but you also get in return. And seeing a person transform as a result of coaching is delightful.

A client had offered me a twelve-month retainer to assist them with strategic planning, coaching of individual managers, facilitating internal workshops and helping them to improve their impact and productivity. The retainer package I put together was for three to four days a month and I worked at a reduced rate as I wouldn't have to market myself for those days. I jumped at the chance because it would mean that I could, with this regular chunk of work, allocate other time to myself, to working on my own projects.

I chose to spend the time developing coaching models for women – and so when I had down-time during this period, I used it to create, read, research, and talk to people. So once again, through choosing work strategically, I was able to do something I was passionate about.

> *Loyalty programs are when you provide a client who is giving you continuous work the benefit of an additional service or reduced rate.*

> *Loyalty programs work best when you come up with innovative ways of meeting their needs.*

Lesson 2: understanding people and their styles

Many organisations are looking for assistance in the restructuring of their businesses, and I enjoy working on this. I knew I could add value to a client, and that they would add value to my business, in time. I really enjoyed the work and as in similar circumstances, had to learn to deal with different egos.

As a consultant, you're expected to come in and make suggestions for change, and sometimes help to implement them. Naturally, that means change and upheaval for the staff, not all of whom are going to be supportive of the changes you're implementing.

Although you can see very clearly as an external person what you want to bring in and implement to improve an organisation, and you can see how those processes are going to help, often others can't see these things as clearly as you. And, in fact, it's often not really the process or the changes that are the issue; instead, it is people's mindsets and egos.

One of the things I learnt from working in this area was how useful personality profiling can be.

There are so many different types of personality profiling – Myers-Briggs and DISC profiles are very well-known, but there are many more in use around the world. The one that I prefer is a mixture of Wilson Learning and Des Hunt.

Ideally, personality profiling needs to be really simple. You may not have as much accuracy – but the idea is that you don't need to analyse a person to death. All you are trying to work out is how to better read that person.

The model that I use has just four basic personality types. Using a clean sheet of paper I map out what I think each of the key managers are, to help me help them. Here is an example of personality types in one company I've worked with.

John was an Owl or analytical. In fact I've realised that's where the word anal comes from! John loved information and research. He wanted to be right, and accuracy is really important to him. This type is not going to go out and buy a television from the first place they go to just because it's a good price. They're going to want to go and get three quotes and then maybe look TVs up on the internet to make sure they are making the right decision.

And so when I work with people like John, I tend to use data. Analytical people really like knowing what's coming. They don't like surprises, they don't want to guess what they are doing tonight; they want to *know* what they're doing tonight in advance so they can put it into their calendar and be prepared for any eventuality.

The type who many feel challenged by is the driver or Eagle. This personality type is often really blunt. They just come out and tell you what they think and what they believe is right and as a result of them being blunt other people think that they're aggressive and can easily be offended by them. Actually, they're not aggressive – it really is just bluntness! And being blunt themselves, if you're blunt with an Eagle he or she won't bat an eyelid. Anne was an Eagle.

Anne tended to make really quick decisions and was far more likely to live by the 80/20 rule: we don't have to get 100 per cent accuracy, if it's 80 per cent right that's okay. They'd rather have something finished quickly and expediently than trying to perfect it.

Anne also loved control. My experience in dealing with Anne was that it was best to give her control and let her make decisions.

When I set up meetings with Anne, rather than say to her 'I want to come and see you and this is the time that I'm available', which gave her no control, I instead gave her control through choice by saying, 'I can come and meet you at 11 am next Tuesday or Thursday afternoon at 4:30, the rest of the week's out for me. What suits you?' There's no need to do more than give them the choices that suit you, but by doing this, I helped Anne to feel in control.

The next type is the amiable, or Dove, which was Janet. Amiable people are good team players. They love reaching consensus with other people and pay a great deal of attention to the opinions of others. So much so that sometimes people look at Doves and think that they don't have an opinion. It's not that they don't have one; they're just trying to get other people's opinions before they share theirs.

What was really important to Janet was relationships. When I dealt with Janet, I usually spent the first fifteen minutes of our hour together talking to her about her family, friends, her recent holiday, her sporting team, etc.

This type of person wants to know that you care, that you can help them, and that you want to have a longer term relationship with them.

And the last type, which I can talk very knowingly about as I am one, is a Peacock, or an expressive person. Marcus liked talking a lot about himself. He was very good at sales and marketing, selling ideas and having a broader vision. When I was dealing with Marcus, I had to consciously work on allowing Marcus to talk more – even though I want to talk a lot about myself – and letting him share his stories.

I think these models are fantastic. I've been using them for a long time and I find that being able to tap in very quickly to others is a great tool. To gain a better understanding of people, and of these models, I would recommend reading Des Hunt's *What Makes People Tick*.

Richard Branson once said that one of the things he loves about working with people is being able to maximise the potential of those he works with. It's all about being versatile and adjusting your communication style to the style of the person you are working with.

One time I was working with the directors of an architecture firm and, using my understanding of this model, it became clear to me that there were a lot of drivers or Eagles in this particular organisation who wanted control. I was able to give them specific projects to work on or get them focused on specific aspects of the project. This strategy worked well during the restructuring process.

Lesson 3: identify your bottom line

During this time I was challenged by being subjected to advances made towards me by a client. It started off very simply, with him asking me about what was going on in my life and how I work and how I spend my time. Then it escalated to him delving into my new relationship. He would ask how the relationship was going, but not only that, he'd ask if I thought it was too soon to get involved, and if perhaps I was better off having some one-night stands or other forms of non-committal relationships. This was when the alarm bells started ringing (yes, I can be slow!). It was with shock that I realised this person was actually coming on to me!

I found this a difficult situation to manage. When you're in a corporation it's different, because you can talk to a colleague or you can talk to someone in your human resources department and work out how you want to deal with it. There are safety nets there for you. But when you are running your own business you don't have that support. I had to sit down and work out what my negotiation strategy was going to be. I'd obviously been privy to a lot of different types of negotiation and one of the things I'd learnt is that you work out your bottom line. Anything below the line is unacceptable and highlights what you will not put up with.

For example, in a relationship it's very clear to me that if somebody hit me that this is well below my bottom line. If that were to happen, I would walk away from the relationship. It would not matter whether we had kids, or what a wonderful person he might be otherwise; it would simply not be acceptable. In the same way I had to work out my bottom line in this instance. I felt that I could continue to work with this person as long as this behaviour stopped. If it didn't, I was prepared to walk away from a fairly large contract as it did not fit with my value-set – and it was below my bottom line.

I sat down with Peter (not his real name) and told him that I found his behaviour unacceptable. Then I gave him a choice. I said: 'We can end the professional relationship now and you can pay out the bill and we'll forget about the rest of the contract, or you can change your behaviour and I can continue to work with you. But you need to know that this behaviour and the questions about my personal life are not acceptable, and neither is coming onto me. He looked shocked that I had called his behaviour, agreed to change it, and apologised.

This was another really important lesson to learn. I'm a very people-oriented person and to me it's important to talk about what you do in your life. But at times people do cross that line – men and women – and you have to be very clear about what you're okay with sharing and what you're not okay with sharing.

> *Is there an area of your life you need to develop your bottom line for?*
>
> *What is acceptable to you?*
>
> *What is not acceptable to you?*

Lesson 4: taking risks

A very large change for me in this year was also making the decision to take the relationship with my soulmate forward – which meant moving interstate. That meant that I had to not only uproot the business but more importantly, leave my parents, my brother, and a lot of my close friends. I'd be leaving a place I'd lived in for ten years, so I went into a place of fear.

I was fearful of starting again, and of losing clients when I moved and would no longer be located in the same city as them. I just didn't know how it would all work. I found myself feeling much the same as I had done in the first couple of months after starting my business.

Initially, after I'd moved, there weren't many phone calls. In fact I didn't really know anyone beside my partner. But rather than get really insecure this time, I felt strong enough to use this time to create things.

One of the things that I had been doing from the very early days of my business was networking, meeting fantastic people. Some of these people had become friends and others had become clients. Gradually my diary had started to get very full – having a coffee with a friend, going into a client meeting, going into a coaching session, meeting another client for a coffee. When I moved states it gave me a chance to reinvent myself and think about my vision for the business. I realised that my diary was going to be pretty clear for a couple of months, and I decided to use that time to work out how I was going to operate going forward. This was a fantastic opportunity – to build up a business by reflection.

> *Well when I started a lot of people in this industry did not have any awareness about our work and the relevance of our product; they just didn't know what we could do. That was difficult. - Ruchi Goel*

This experience reminded me of a story I was told early on in my career. A Japanese manufacturing plant ran a competition amongst their employees to see who could come up with the best safety idea. They were offered a substantial prize. The people entering typically came up with ideas such as places they could put hand-rails or suggestions for new walkways. The person who won the award, however, had decided to create a two-metre-square Japanese garden in the middle of the plant. The idea was that if the workers stop and reflect, there will be fewer workplace injuries. We all can apply this to our own business, we need time to reflect also – not just when things go wrong, but simply to allow ourselves space and time. This should be proactively and regularly built into your diary.

Lesson 5: using reflection

When something goes wrong our tendency is to go in there thinking 'Right, I've got to fix this; there's been a mistake, there's been an injury, I've got to fix it'. When a customer complains, I think: 'I want to fix it'. When somebody gives us negative feedback in a personal relationship, we want to fix it. But in all this fixing, it's easy to lose sight of the bigger questions. Why are things going wrong in the first place? It's so important to take time out for reflection. Someone I met told me that I may be seen as a 'feminist' by mainly working with women and I took that view without working out that he was not representative of the people I worked with and that most people probably wouldn't see me that way at all.

What became clear to me in that time was that my fears were unfounded. I was scared of the massive change I was experiencing both in my personal and my professional life. Some of those fears were related to stepping into what could potentially be a long-term relationship and also the new role of being a step-mum. But the fears surfaced in professional relationships as well.

> *Do you take time to reflect? Did you know 0.6 per cent of your week equates to an hour of reflection time?*
>
> *Can you allow yourself 0.6 per cent of a week?*
>
> *When can you start? Build this into your diary each week.*

As I continued to reflect, it became clear to me that I wanted to have a part of the business that was just dedicated to women and was marketed that way. I wanted to have more women working with me. So I decided to invest in those areas over the next three months. I started to use some of the funds that I had available while the revenue was a bit slow and I asked myself 'how do I learn more about women?' I decided to attain my coaching qualifications in this period to realise the dream.

In Australia at present, there are no qualifications needed to be a coach and unfortunately that means every man, woman and their dog can become a coach. My belief is eventually coaching qualifications will come in as the practice becomes more and more established. However, at that time I did a lot of research and found a US-based organisation which does accreditation once a year in Australia. I invested a substantial amount of money to gain coaching qualifications through them. They had all the models and over thirty years of research that I could tap into. That really excited me as I could use this knowledge to help others.

I met some very like-minded people doing the course and had some profound realisations. I realised that in the same way that women like going to women doctors, it was very likely that many women would like going to women coaches.

The other thing that I invested in was a women's workshop. I'd attended numerous courses and different training camps, but I'd never attended an all women's workshop. The wonderful learning from this workshop was about aligning and connecting your heart, your soul and your mind. And I learnt so much from this workshop – for example that through dance and expression of self you can release a lot of emotion – that I started to include forms of this in my own workshops.

I am still learning to go back and align everything I do with my heart, with feelings rather than thoughts, and realising that whenever I felt good about something it would always have a much better outcome compared to just doing things that seemed sensible, for example, getting more exposure in terms of marketing or advertising.

When I had down time
I used it to create, read,
research, and talk to people.

Chapter 6

Year 5:
dream the dream

Celebrate your achievements ❦ Ask, believe and
receive ❦ Be careful what you wish for ❦ Working
with affirmations ❦ Redefine your vision

We must be the change we wish to see.
— MK Ghandi

I n year five my first and best accomplishment was to survive the stats! The 80/20 rule does not apply to me, I remember thinking – I am not part of the 80 per cent of businesses that do not survive beyond that point. I'm going to be part of the surviving 20 per cent and that in itself feels like a large achievement.

Could I have done things better? Absolutely. But would I continue to do some of the things that I did in exactly the same way? Absolutely. So this called for a celebration. When we achieve our milestones in business, we have to celebrate that success.

> *Self doubt is number one. I mean you have this inner belief that you can do it, but until you start to prove it to yourself, you wonder, can I really do it? And I overcame that by making sure I celebrated the small wins. I just think that a lot of people in this world celebrate the big wins, but forget about the small victories. You need to understand those small wins, and why they occurred also, because they are so important. I don't believe in the word failure. – Julian Burton*

A wise man I worked with a long time ago, Trevor, would buy a plant every time he won a significant job or achieved a milestone. As his home office faced the garden, he could see his rewards each time he looked out of the window and identify that camellia which was for winning that engineering contract and so on. Personally, I love buying a nice piece of jewellery! So that's how I celebrate – with a bit of retail therapy or a massage.

> *How do you celebrate when you achieve your milestones? Why not do it in a tangible way – so each time you put on that pair of shoes or water your beautiful garden, you have an automatic memory of a success!*

Lesson 1: attract positivity

I have a rule that if three people tell me about a person, a book, CD or DVD within a short space of time, it is a message to go and do something about it. One such experience was a DVD called *The Secret* which had accompanying CDs and books, created by Rhonda Byrne. It was mentioned to me three times within a week by three unrelated people around Australia. It was my calling.

Although like most books, I did not agree with everything in it (just like you will not agree with everything in this book), a lot of it did make sense to me. It reinforced the power of positive thinking. It is based around the concept of the Law of Attraction, which simply states that you attract what you think and feel. Your life is a testimony to what you have attracted. As Byrne says, 'Whatever it is you are feeling is a perfect reflection of what is in the process of becoming!' This creative process was one of the things that I loved the most about it. It provided an easy set of guidelines to create whatever you wanted in life. I interpreted it as three simple steps: ask, believe, receive.

I think [my success] is just down to my determination, my focus and my organisation. I am very goal orientated and I keep to my intentions, having both small goals and big goals, and I get help when I need to.
– Kea Dent

Ask

The first step is to *ask* – make a command to the universe so it can respond. Be clear about what you want.

There were times in my business when I just completely floundered. Although I thought I was doing the right thing and knew I was working really hard, I wasn't clear about what I really wanted and I was full of mixed messages. This comes back to vision. If you're not clear in your vision, then the Law of Attraction cannot bring you what you want. It brings you instead the results of the state of confusion that you are in.

Whether you call it the Law of Attraction or your vision, it's essentially the same thing as I see it. It's about gaining clarity about what you want.

Believe

Step two is to *believe* that it – the thing you want – is already here. I find this challenging myself and through experience can say that many women find it difficult to wholeheartedly believe – whether that be believing in themselves, or simply believing fully in the power and worth of their vision.

Whether it's a highly profitable business, confidence, perfect skin, a soulmate – it's all there. The work for you is to act as if you've already received it. I often use this approach with people in my work. It's often referred to as affirmations or positive visualisation.

In my work, often those who want to get up to that next level tell me 'I want to be the manager or director or CEO', and my answer is always, 'Well, act like you're there'. I don't mean throwing your weight around; but I do mean acting with great confidence, being true to yourself.

If you believe and act,
the universe will start to
correspond with what you
really want.

If you believe and act, the universe will start to correspond with what you really want and you will start to make decisions with the kind of personal power and energy that you would were you in that role already. You won't spend all your energy on others. And, you know what else? Acting with that kind of power and energy will get you noticed in a positive way.

It's about acting as if you are already there, and the effect is that you are putting the intention out all the time. You have to start believing in order for what you wish for to be delivered. If you don't believe in yourself – or if it doesn't show – why would anyone else believe in you?

When you act this way, don't think about the extra money or the career path or who in the organisation is not doing the right thing. You need to be purely focused on creating what you want, working with that intention.

> *The universe acts as a mirror and the Law of Attraction mirrors back whatever you're thinking about the most.*
>
> *Naturally this works for both positive and negative intentions, so be clear on what you are creating!*
>
> *As the old saying goes, 'Be careful what you wish for'.*

Here's a very simple example. I popped down to the supermarket to get milk for the clients that were arriving one morning at my office. I had to park my car in a loading zone as there was no other parking available. As I was feeling frustrated driving around, I remember thinking to myself, if I park in the loading zone, I hope I don't get a parking ticket.

I parked in the loading zone, ran inside in my high heels and was back out within three minutes … and guess what? There was a parking ticket for $45. That was expensive milk!

I was mad at myself. I understood the principle but still attracted the ticket to myself. Then I realised that my thought was focused on 'I don't want a parking ticket' and that is exactly what I got because the universe heard 'I want a parking ticket'!

The thoughts have to be carefully worded to ensure you're emitting the right frequency to bring the right people into your life. I used to be an ANALytical engineer, so I have to test things before I believe, and that is exactly what I've been doing. The experiment is working – what I am trying to manifest is coming into alignment. The bigger goals that I've been setting, even the BHAG – Big Hairy Audacious Goals - are starting to be realised.

> *Have you thought about your BHAG?*
>
> *What would you do if you had no limits?*
>
> *What are you creating in your life?*
>
> *Which creations are you happy with, and which would you like to change?*

How do you believe something that isn't true? You just do it. Repeat it as if it is true. For example, if you tell a child that he or she is fantastic over and over again, he or she starts to believe it. In the same fashion, if you tell a child that he or she is no good and a pain over and over again, he or she will believe that as well.

As a human, I am unable to apply these principles 100 per cent of the time but the aim is to consciously become more aware of what I am creating.

Affirmations are a good way to believe what you already have. They work like:

1. They must start with an 'I'. You can only affirm for yourself – there's really no point saying, 'if James did x, I would feel better'. Instead, try: 'I love the support I get from James'.

2. They must be positive. Rather than 'If I was less fat, I would feel good', instead affirm 'I am healthy', or 'I enjoy my healthy strong

body', and even if you know you need to lose weight, the positive affirmation will make you feel better about the body you have – and perhaps also give you the willpower, for instance, to go to the gym!

3. They must be present tense. When what you're actually thinking is, 'When I go on holiday to Thailand, I will be less stressed'. Instead, try affirming: 'I am relaxed now'.

Lance Armstrong's book *It's Not About the Bike* shared not only his passion for riding but also the way he used affirmations to get rid of cancer from his body in spite of the dire predictions from medical experts. I particularly remember him discussing his approach to the painful vomiting that came as a result of his cancer treatment. This amazing man chose to see the vomiting as a symbol of him getting rid of his cancer.

Let me use the example of this book. I had about 10 per cent of this book written and then I learnt from the publisher that my deadlines were going to have to change radically. What the ...!

I had no idea how I was going to do it. I just knew that I *was* going to do it. So I used the process I've shared with you above. My affirmation was 'my book is published' and I visualised doing book signings around various cities. I used my meditation and relaxation techniques to believe that this was true even if it was not. And I got it done.

I wasn't even sure if the publisher at that stage would take this project on but I kept affirming that this book is going to go out and influence millions of women and their families, which was my vision for it.

I did have my doubts at times. One night I was writing at 11 pm. I don't generally work after 6 pm and I felt that I couldn't do it. Rather than continue that night, I stopped and repeated my affirmation and visualised the book signings. And you know what? Here you are reading this book, so it works!

Receive

Step three of the process is to *receive* and act as if it's already here. A good way is to have gratitude for what you already have.

When you start to turn your different dreams into reality you realise that you can start to work on bigger dreams and then on converting them into bigger realities. This is one of the greatest learnings I have had in the last year.

But there is action required. It won't come by just sitting there! And sometimes it is not the easiest path. As humans we have a tendency to take the path of least resistance. I can't just sit back and say I want a million dollars and expect that million dollars to come to me. I want to ask for that million dollars, believe that I have it already and put things into action in terms of how I create that million dollars. All this time I am affirming and visualising. Once I have done that, I then have to receive.

Once when I thought I wanted to be earning a certain amount of money I realised that it clashed with wanting to have weekends off, wanting to spend quality time with my partner and family and also having time to grow, reflect and recharge. I had to revise my wish then, so the intent was broader, more about I am happy and content in the now, appreciating my wealth of good experiences, times with loved ones and the ease with which money flows into my life.

I used this process to invite my soulmate into my life. Many people want their soulmate but have not done enough work on themselves to be able to receive that person into their lives, or to get beyond the stage of expecting that the soulmate will be perfect – they're not and yet they are!

One day I decided I was ready to *receive* my soulmate.

In order to manifest a soulmate into my life, I created a list. The top of my list said 'soulmate' and the list had nine characteristics. Those characteristics were wide and varied, including friendly in terms of personality; somebody who would be supportive of my growth, both personal and professional; someone with a great sense of humour; and someone who loved both my ups and my downs. And guess what? He arrived, he actually arrived and met all nine criteria.

> *Sketch who you want to bring into your life – whether it be a staff member, a customer or a soulmate.*
>
> *List the characteristics that you want them to have.*
>
> *Put it out there, believe and then receive.*

Lesson 2: make things happen for yourself

You might have picked up on something I said above about affirmations. I mentioned wishing to make a certain amount of money and then working out how that was going to happen. Yes, I asked and believed; but I also put practical steps in process.

When I moved states, I wanted to meet some nice people so I made a list. I joined the Hunter Youth Mentoring Collaborative (www.hymc. com.au) Advisory Board. I wanted to extend my expertise in the support and development and mentoring of sometimes disadvantaged young people. I love the idea that through a mentoring relationship these young people can access guidance for their careers and personal life.

What lies behind us and what lies before us are small matters to what lies within us. – Ralph Waldo Emerson

Continually self-educate, do courses and take education opportunities such as business coaching. You really can't afford to rest on your laurels. – Janelle Gerrard

Through working in this capacity I've met many amazing people. One is a young man called Victor, who as a result of his involvement with the program has stayed away from drugs and now has an apprenticeship. And I'm discussing writing a book in collaboration with a friend from the advisory board. So the experiences, both of seeing the transformation in the young people, and giving myself more of a firm footing in my new home, have been wonderful.

As work has started to flow from interstate and overseas, I am away from home more. Work–life balance is extremely important to me and my husband (yes, I married my soulmate), and we have set a ground rule of not being away from each other for more than two nights a week, on average. That may work out to mean no travel one week and three or four days in the next week. So that has forced me to develop my bottom lines personally and professionally.

When opportunities come in, we weigh them up against our careers, kids and life. It is impossible, as business continues to grow, to be able to chase every opportunity that comes in. We need to look at the opportunities and ask: which line up with my vision, values and principles? Where am I going to get the biggest result for the time I put in?

This year, I was approached by a television station to host a business show. I wasn't sure if this was something that I really wanted to do but as I started to investigate, I realised that the audience was going to be large. I had never thought of doing television but this opportunity has come to help manifest my vision of being able to positively influence billions of people and their families.

I am still learning to work on the business. Michael Gerber, author of *The E-Myth*, and considered to be one of the world's leading small-business gurus, says, 'If we're always working in the business then essentially we've just got a job'.

Entrepreneur and bestselling author Brad Sugars calls the J.O.B. 'just over broke'. I just didn't want to do that. I wanted to create a business where the business is able to be functioning when I am not in it myself 100 percent of the time. It has taken me a long time to learn how to manifest that and work out what I need to put into place for that to happen.

So once again, I have invited people and experts in to help me grow. One woman, Vicky, has come into my life, suggesting that I record my speaking engagements and make them into a DVD. That made so much sense!

My vision is to inspire, challenge and transform a billion people to believe in themselves. Now that I have become really clear on what I want, the Universe has started to align itself to helping me achieve that BHAG (big hairy audacious goal).

The medium – whether it is speaking, working in the media, workshops or writing – I no longer feel tied into. I just want to get out there and change the world and create my legacy.

So what is your vision?

I wanted to create a business where the business is able to be functioning, when I am not in it myself, 100 per cent of the time as a true business should!

Chapter 7

your personal plan and inspirations

Inspiration ❖ Vision ❖ Tools ❖
Using language ❖ Powerful quotes

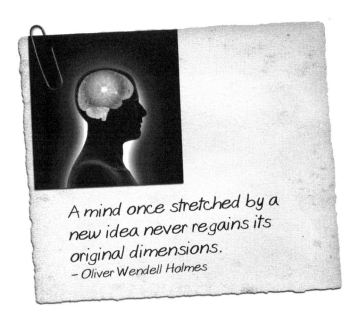

A mind once stretched by a new idea never regains its original dimensions.
– Oliver Wendell Holmes

T his chapter is for you to use as a resource and a source of inspiration, helping you during your transformation.

Many people want to get to a transformation workshop, speaking event, or the help of a professional business coach but don't have the resources, whether time or financial. What I have created is a simple 'self coaching' guide that will help you uncover what your passion@work is. And in the abundance mentality, it is free for you. For further free articles on this topic have a look at www.shivani.com.au

Find some time for reflection and some silent time. Take a minimum of about an hour a week, just for yourself. Don't have a laptop or mobile near you. All you'll need is this book, a piece of paper, and a pen, and ask yourself the questions that follow.

Good luck in your own journey of transformation!

Your passion@work plan

My passion
What work would I do if money was no object?

What do I get really passionate about?

Am I working in my areas of passion?

If not, why not? What are my fears?

How can I overcome my fears?

What small action can I take to overcome my fears? *(For example, if you're thinking of a career change, why not try some work experience or work in this area part-time.)*

If I am ready to move into areas of my passion, what are my short term (1–3 months) and medium term (3–12 months) goals?

Short term

Medium term

Attracting positive people

Who am I not getting along with or having confrontations with, at present?

_____

_____

_____

_____

What kinds of differences do we have in our behaviour and personalities?

_____

_____

_____

_____

What kind of people do I want to bring into my life? *(These can be staff, mentors or anyone else.)*

_____

_____

_____

Many people walk around the edge of a problem rather than facing it, as that may be confronting. And many of us don't get high on confrontation.

But having robust conversations must not be seen as being aggressive. Why not try taking the following actions:

Get your intention clear. Ask yourself: What am I trying to achieve? How do I want to come across?

If the idea of bringing something up makes you worry, it is usually a sign that you must bring it up. Think of it as coming from a place of love rather than a place of fear. If you come from fear, you may attack. If you come from love, you are trying to get to the outcome you desire. What is the outcome you would like?

What is the other person's intention? Ask them for what they are trying to achieve at the beginning of the meeting.

Where are the gaps in what the other person desires and what you desire?

How do you take the emotion out of this conversation?

How can you become more accepting of them?

Continue to be true to yourself and just be 'you' in this interaction.

Working with fear

Fear is normal. When you make a change, you may experience fear but you cannot live in it. Instead, live with it and work through it.

What am I fearful of right now?

Where does this fear come from?

What can I do to reduce or alleviate the fear?

How will I feel when I am not operating from fear?

Marketing myself

What are some of my best assets or characteristics?

When I go to a function, how do I introduce myself?

Who could I be marketing to ... but don't?

How could I approach someone I don't know?

What is one area that I have thought would be a great way to market myself and my business?

What actions can I put in place to try this?

Get help

Which area do I need the most help in? *(This could be staff, systems or anything else.)*

Who do I know that could help me?

How do I approach them?

What have they suggested?

How do I implement the changes in my work or personal life?

....

....

....

Communicate assertively

Am I generally passive or aggressive in my communication? Or am I in
the middle of the road – assertive?

....

....

....

....

Am I different at home compared to work? If so, why?

....

....

....

Who am I passive with?

....

....

....

Who am I aggressive with?

Where do I feel the most comfortable, where I can be assertive?

What do I need to change in my language or communication style to move towards being assertive?

Taking risks

Am I good at taking risks?

If I am not, why not?

If I am, why?

What calculated risk would I like to take but have not done so yet?

What can I do to put this into action?

My personal plan

My body

What are some areas where I feel negative about my health or body at the moment?

....

....

....

Which one area do I want to work on today?

....

....

....

How am I feeling about this area?
In the circle below, draw words and images that come into your mind when thinking about that area.

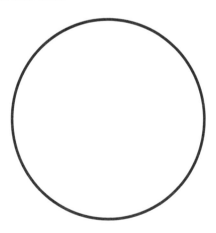

What is one small action I can take today to change this?

For example if you feel fat, work on replacing one unhealthy habit today with a healthy one. It may be as simple as eating an apple instead of a chocolate biscuit. The rest of it you don't need to change today. Just take it one step at a time.

Keep a journal for two weeks, noting down what you have done and how you feel.

While keeping your journal, write an affirmation to change your negative thoughts and emotions. Remember an affirmation is positive, phrased as if it is already true, and starts with I. For example, I am attractive.

Repeat this affirmation four or five times a day for the two weeks you keep your journal.

WEEK ONE

Sunday

Monday

Tuesday

Wednesday

Thursday

Friday

Saturday

WEEK TWO

Sunday

Monday

Tuesday

Wednesday

Thursday

Friday

Saturday

Reflection after two weeks:

Am I feeling better about this?

....

....

....

If not, what other area of my body do I need to work on?

Repeat the circle exercise above.

....

....

....

Continue to work on this.

My money

Do I feel positive or negative when I think about money?

Do I have enough to live the lifestyle I wish to?

If not, how much more do I need?

What is blocking me from earning the money I want and deserve?

What barriers in my mind are stopping me from doing this?

For example, you may have the mindset that you don't deserve to earn $80,000. This mindset needs to be changed.

What action am I going to take?

For example, you could look for another job. Or you could work on changing your mindset so that you don't limit your views about money.

And remember that money is good. It is easy. There is an abundance of it for everyone. Do not read conflicting information – aim to keep your mind positive about money.

My relationships

Who really annoys me or hurts me?

....

....

....

What past hurts do I need to let go of?

When thinking about people involved in past hurts, send them love. This may feel hard but close your eyes and picture them. See them as someone who is a little child fighting for their needs. Forgive them and send them love. Afterwards, reflect on how it felt.

....

....

....

....

What are some of my behaviours that I have picked up from my parents, siblings or friends that I really don't like about myself?

....

....

....

....

How would I like to behave instead?

What small actions am I going to put in place to change my behaviour?

Who do I love that I need to act differently towards?

Our tendency is to think all our beliefs are ours because we don't spend time on reflecting which ones we've picked up along the way from others and whether we are really happy with them.

My mind

What am I thankful for today? What do I already have that I need to acknowledge and have gratitude for?

How much time am I spending living in the future or the past versus the present?

What can I do to live more in the present? Are there any negative thoughts that I could just let go of?

What are some of the things I have failed at?

Change your view on a failure you have had. Relabel it as a *lesson*.

Who do I feel I am in competition with?

Work on changing your concept of competition. There is enough for everyone. There is no need for competition.

A meditation

Find somewhere at home you can sit quietly for ten minutes, without phones or other interruptions. Now start to breathe in and out. As you breathe in, take the breath deep into your belly until you can feel it move out. Then slowly exhale.

Repeat this five times until your body begins to slow down.

Now think about something you have wanted in your life for a long time. Start to feel the abundance – feel that it is already there.

As you start to imagine that you have that thing, person or relationship in your life already, feel good about it. Feel like there is nothing in your way, nothing that will not allow you to have it. Start to say thanks for letting me have …

Then slowly begin to focus on your breath again. Breathe in deep into your belly and then exhale. Repeat this another five times.

Then slowly come back to where you are sitting and open your eyes.

How do you feel?

The interviews

You may have noticed throughout this book that, as much as I've been inspired by the amazing books I've read, I've also been inspired by the many wonderful, energetic, driven people I've met. Among those are the people I interviewed for this book.

The top traits of a great business leader, according to the interviewees, were:

Have great work ethic, drive, passion and determination

Be creative and access knowledge formal or informal as much as possible, it helps you continuously stay fresh and inspired

Have good people skills

Be yourself and know that your personality is a big part of your business

Be focused, with good attention to details

Main advice from interviewees:

Be actively engaged in continuous learning

Have goals and a plan, and stick to it

Have systems and attention to detail

Be organised

Have an attitude of gratitude and giving

Enjoy and have fun

The interviewees

Scott Anthony – PureENVY Jewellery

After nearly twenty years working in the jewellery industry, designing and manufacturing, award-winning jewellery designer Scott Anthony opened pureENVY Jewellery to the public. Scott's work sells to clients around Australia and from overseas.

Kylie Armstrong

Kylie Armstrong is a herbalist and masseuse. Her passion is to help women with infertility through natural processes. She is achieving enormous success for her clients who can face anything from bad backs to cancer to infertility.

Julian Burton – Julian Burton Burns Trust

Julian Burton's diverse experiences include pursuing a career in professional sport, working as an educator and surviving the Bali bombings. He is now a professional speaker empowering people to take action.

Jenny Carmuciano – JLC Consulting

Jenny Carmuciano has been involved in recruitment, assessment centres and facilitation for organisations such as GIO/Suncorp, Telstra Graduate Recruitment, Vic Roads Graduate Recruitment, Coles Myer, Connex, Linfox and Toyota. Jenny has also taught Business Studies at a tertiary level.

Kea Dent – Kea Dent & Associates

Kea became involved in the medical device industry running a successful medical manufacturer. Kea has an MBA, and was the 2002 winner of the South Australian Telstra Business Woman of the Year in the private sector category. In 2003, she was a State Finalist in the Entrepreneur of the Year Awards.

Katrina Finlayson – Dragonfly Software

Katrina Finlayson started her business with her business partner Shane. They offer custom software development services. Their vision is to lead the way in delivering a higher standard of customer service and business value outcomes.

Janelle Gerrard – Design Change

Janelle has over twenty years experience in design, marketing and advertising in Sydney. Since establishing Design Change she has created memorable graphics for businesses such as Andor, Jo Coffey Training Connection, Waratah Engineering, Trans Tasman Masters Games, ARCHI, Villa Clone, and Bishop Grove Wines. Her aim is to provide her clients with professionalism, creativity and value.

Jennie Groom – Jennie Groom Photography

Jennie Groom has received many awards at national and state level including awards for both Commercial and Illustrative Photographer of the Year. Her work has also been accepted into two Fuji ACMP Australian Photographers' Collections.

Abbie Martin – Lifestyle Elements

Lifestyle Elements acts as a personal assistant, personal shopper and all-round organiser. Founder and Principal Lifestyle Manager, Abbie Martin is also Vice-President of the International Concierge & Errand Association's Australia and New Zealand Chapter.

Nick Palousis – Natural Edge Project

Nick Palousis, past member of The Natural Edge Project, a sustainability think tank, has been awarded the William T Southcott Scholarship. This prestigious scholarship is offered to an outstanding PhD student to undertake research in Advanced Manufacturing Engineering or a related discipline.

Simone Preston – Business Women Connect

Business Women Connect, a regular networking platform for business-women, has been specifically designed by Simone Preston utilising her extensive business and networking skills. Simone wants to provide businesswomen with networking opportunities and motivation.

Mark Priadko – ABFA Pty Ltd

Mark Priadko has worked in Treasury and Finance at a state government level as General Manager, Government Accounting and Reporting. Over eleven years, Mark has developed expertise in reporting, analysis, advice, policies and standards in relation to government finances. Mark also speaks on financial management to government forums, CPA congresses and CPA discussion groups.

Katrina Webb – Kwik Kat Enterprises

Katrina Webb is recognised for her outstanding success as a Paralympic athlete. She is also a sought after motivational/inspirational keynote speaker and runs her own business, Kwik Kat Enterprises. Kwik Kat Enterprises specialises in team-building workshops and health and wellbeing programs.

Share with us

If there are any stories that have had an effect on you, or if you would like to share your story or that of someone you know, we would love to hear from you. Please contact us at **www.shivani.com.au**

The author

Shivani was born in India but spent most of her childhood in a remote part of South Australia. A qualified engineer, she completed an MBA by the age of 27, before working as a senior manager with BHP Billiton

After a life-changing trip to Nepal, Shivani left the corporate world to pursue her passion to create her own business coaching and development company. Shivani translated her passion for helping others achieve their goals into a successful small business specialising in the development and growth of business and business women. She has since worked with a wide range of businesses from sole traders through to some of Australia's largest companies. She is also in demand as a business coach, public speaker and board member.

Shivani has won multiple business awards including the 'Telstra Young Business Woman of the Year' and 'Achiever of the Year for Enterprising Women'. Her work with universities has seen her made an honorary member of the Golden Key, alongside the likes of Bill Clinton and Ian Thorpe.

As well as being a certified business and executive coach, she is a member of the Australian Institute of Company Directors and of the Australian Institute of Management. Shivani is also a Fairfax small business columnist and presenter of the SBS TV show on start up businesses *Risking It All*.